ABOVE AND BEYOND

Making SenseOf Your Destiny Journey

Andrew Mudolo

DEDICATION

I dedicate the book to every person out there who has stood true to
their dreams. This world has been beautified and developed by
people who believed in the beauty of their dreams. This book is for
the next generation of dreamers, both old and young
God bless.

CONTENTS

vi

FOREWARD

You've probably heard of the great author and incredible business entrepreneur Helen Keller, who became blind, deaf, and mute as a result of an illness when she was only eighteen months old. She fought through her limitations and became a powerful, remarkable woman who impacted her generation. In her old age, a news anchor interviewed her. Communicating his questions to her through braille, he asked, "Miss. Keller, what is far worse than being blind, deaf and mute?" she paused for a moment and in her unique way of talking she said, "what is worse than being blind, deaf and mute is having sight without vision".

Helen Keller in one of her quotes made this profound statement, "when one door of happiness closes another opens but often we look so long at the closed door that we do not see the one that has opened for us."

The door of her sight was shut the door of her speech was shut, the door of her hearing was shut, but she began to focus on the small door that was opened (learning to read by help of her teacher Miss.

Sullivan, through symbols recognition in her palms,) and seized it and became a great woman in history.

The most significant loss in life on earth is not a loss of sight, a spouse, child, a house, business but the loss of belief. When one loses faith, a person loses hope, and when hope is lost, then the purpose is canceled and life loses meaning and explanation.

In this profound book "ABOVE AND BEYOND," Andrew Mudolo draws incredible lessons from the biblical character Joseph and inspire us to pursue the dream that God has placed in our hearts and further teaches us several practical tools such as:

-	How to Conceive a dream or vision from God

-	How to Believe what you have Conceived regardless of challenges

-	How to Protect what you have Conceived

-	How to Deliver what you have Conceived

-	Making into reality what you have Conceived in your environment for generation impact.

By Maurice Mvula – Life Coach and Mentor

INTRODUCTION

There is a man whose name became synonymous with the living embodiment of evil. He inspired others to commit heinous crimes and was himself responsible for many brutal murders. Charles Manson is said to have turned out as a murderous cult leader following a childhood of pain. Manson was born to a teenage alcoholic prostitute and an absentee father. He found himself in trouble throughout his childhood, and the results of how he turned out are evidenced by some 35 killings he and his cult 'The Family' carried out.

On the other side of the coin, you read of a man called Abraham Lincoln who failed in business and was driven to the edge–he had a nervous breakdown. As if that was not enough; he was defeated eight times in elections before becoming president of USA.

I want to show you that failure to make sense of life's experience can make a beast out of a saint.

But if one master challenges and hardships of life, they can rise to become better men, men like Nelson Mandela, who after serving

27 years imprisonment became the first black president of South Africa. In a continent where leaders often hold on to power till death, Mandela willingly handed over the Presidency. That is a man who made sense out of his imprisonment.

The name Oprah Winfrey is celebrated among women world over as an icon of hope and affluence. What is not apparent is that behind the polished Oprah are scars of a very painful past. Her teenage parents separated after her birth, leaving Oprah to be raised by her grandmother. Beyond poverty, Oprah faced other hardships. Her life is punctuated by episodes of pain and misery; she lived in continuous trauma and crisis. Abandoned by her parents, Oprah grew up in the care of people that took advantage of her vulnerability. At the age of nine, she was raped by one of her relatives, and as though that was not enough, she faced continuous sexual harassment by another two of her relatives. As a 14-year-old, she became pregnant and gave birth to a son who died shortly after that.

The traumatic experiences helped develop in her a fighting spirit that has seen her exile to become the queen of daytime TV. Behind her glory lays a story of a gray childhood.

Oprah resolved that "I will overcome everything and be the best that I can ever be." Well, that's the winning formula.

The secret to discover is that never allow your pain to damage you permanently, but use your pain as a springboard that launches you into your dreams and destiny. It is a fact that you will go through pain in your life, but how you choose to respond to it is all up to you. And the choice you make is what makes or breaks you.

Oprah went above and beyond her childhood pain and misery to owning her own Cable Network. Against all the odds, Oprah pushed through her grief and poverty to become the first African American TV correspondent in Nashville at age 19. Today, Ninety-nine percent of homes in America and sixty-four countries of the world listen to it and watch it and thus ensure her annual income of $170 million. In 2013 Oprah's net worth was estimated at $2.9 billion.

Oprah had to relive her childhood pain when she battled with excess weight and her inability to break the wrong relationships with the opposite sex. It was as though a ghost from her past had come to haunt her. Still, Oprah went on strong. Oprah had to muster the courage to go 'Above and Beyond' childhood abandonment and sexual abuse to remodel her life. Her story inspires many people today because she persevered; she made sense out of her childhood abuse.

The fact is that every product results from a process of works done on raw materials. We have to realize that a dream envisioned is just but a piece of raw material and if not processed, will be buried, buried and forgotten despite all its potential of being a product of blessing to humanity.

Many people throw off their dreams simply because they encounter an obstacle. For instance, verbal obstacles of negative speech and criticism can at times if not well handled could be deadly immobilizers of all advance motion towards dream realization.

Beyond verbal, obstacles come in different packages and sizes, with all sorts of colors; in the case of Oprah, those obstacles came in the form of abandonment and sexual abuse.

Your obstacles may be unique to you, but through the stories of other people and their experiences, you too can muster the courage to go 'Above and Beyond' those obstacles.

Always remember this—when you hit a dead-end still realize that just past that dead-end is the point of start of new life. Frequently, people fail mainly not to a lack of strength but rather to a lack of will. If you can only hold on, persist a little longer, your breakthrough is nearing every passing moment of endurance.

The story of Joseph in the bible is one that has fascinated me most in my life's journey with regard to God's purpose for my life. For many years I have taught and preached from this story with tremendous testimonies from hearers.

I remember being asked to share a word with an assembly of youths. I felt impressed to share this story. In attendance was the patron of this youth group, the man was a retired army officer, over sixty years of age.

He made one remarkable statement that I have treasured in my ministry since; he said: "young man you have caused me to dream again."

My purpose and prayer in writing this book are that many young and older people alike will join this sixty-year plus retired army officer in dreaming again. There are many things you might have gone or will go through that have the potential of numbing all your efforts of realizing your dreams, but you've got to be strong. You can't afford to give up.

The world is waiting for you to manifest, to reveal the great blessing you have to offer. I can trace the inspiration to write this story from my high school days as I served God in the Scripture Union at Kabwe High School in the central province town of Kabwe in Zambia.

I can't even begin to count the number of times that I have preached and taught this story, given motivation talks based on the life story of this bible character. It has been with great pleasure that I read and talk about this story. I hope that in this book, I'll be able to communicate the lessons I have learned and preached. Like Oprah, many people can relate to the story of Joseph, but unfortunately many people end up as frustrated failures because they can't or have failed to muster the lessons of courage, perseverance, and forgiveness. I believe every young person needs to master this biography of Joseph for the encouragement on their own life's journey to their dream. And surely every adult needs to revise the story of Joseph to renew and revitalize their dreams and hopes amid life's impediments and hardships.

God never promises a smooth sail, but he guarantees a safe arrival

When Does the Pain and Hurt Stop?

Now you might be saying, "I was molested by my father and have been a victim of repeated rape. I have been through counseling, and I'm on medication. I am now thirty-something years and have no passion, no sex drive whatsoever. I have never really had a healthy relationship, been through a painful divorce and the social labeling that results from a failed marriage. I'm tired of the pain and rejection of the people I trusted. I want a normal life you might be saying". And every time you want to make progress in reclaiming your life, you find that the past is revived by one happening or another. The big question is, when does the pain of your experiences stop?"

Well, the blunt truth is that THE PAIN AND HURT STOP WHEN YOU DECIDE TO STOP BEING A VICTIM.

In this book, you will learn to see yourself as being higher than your experiences in life. You must realize that all things are possible if you never give up! The unpopular truth is that the greater our aims, goals, dreams, aspirations, or ambitions, the greater the obstacles to their achievement.

Booker T. Washington said, "I have learned that success is to be measured not so much by the position that one has reached in life as by the obstacles, which he has overcome while trying to succeed."

Allow me to share another story with you.

One day I was sitting on the balcony looking at the birds chirping away, and I remembered Jesus words, I prayed; "God, how can you take care of the birds and not me?" Then it hit me; there are 24 hours in a day - sitting in depression with your curtains closed, no-one's going to give you back those 24 hours. Before you know, it's a week, a month, a year wasted away. That was a harsh reality.

You see, I had a terrible breakdown. I felt let down by God; I felt let down by everybody. I couldn't believe that people could be laughing, going out and just going about life. I crashed, said Terry Gobanga, a Kenyan pastor who was gang-raped on her wedding day; yes; gang-raped on her wedding day.

The episodes in her life led people to think she was a witch or probably under some curse. Coming back from escorting a friend who was taking a necktie to her fiancé earlier that morning of her wedding, Terry fell into the hands of some terrible people.

As she walked past a guy sitting on the bonnet of a car - suddenly he grabbed her from behind and dumped me in the back seat.

There were two more men inside, and they drove off. It all happened in a fraction of a second Terry recounts.

Removing the cloth placed over her mouth, she managed to scream, but the men threatened to kill her if she did not keep quiet. The men took turns to rape her, and she felt as if she was going to die. With much resolve, she kept fighting for her life, and when one of the men took the gag out of her mouth, she bit his manhood. The man screamed in pain, and one of them stabbed her in the stomach.

The car was still in motion when one of them opened the door and threw her out. Terry was injured and bled badly. The men had driven far away, and now Terry was miles from home, outside Nairobi—more than six hours had passed since her abduction. Meanwhile, at the All Saints Cathedral when the bride didn't show up, people started wondering—Did she change her mind? Rumors of her absence started going around. As for her parents, they felt worried and started panicking. When the thought of her changing her mind came up, those who knew her well said: "No, it's so unlike her, what happened?" they wondered.

According to doctors, the knife to her stomach went to deep to her womb, and she wouldn't be able to have children. Her Dream of Motherhood was shattered.

Another test followed her; the police never caught the rapists. She went to the Police station and inspected line-ups for the perpetrators but all to no avail. Line-up after line-up but she couldn't recognize any of the men. As expected, it hurt her more each time she went to the police. She said that it set back her recovery - it was like taking ten steps forward, then 20 back.

To move on beyond the incident, she went back to the police station and said: "You know what, I'm done. I want to leave it." That is what I call passing the test of forgiveness.

Her fiancé Harry kept saying he still wanted to marry her despite all that had happened to her.

I felt I had let him down—it was painful to look him in the eye, she said. Another rape survivor read her story, met up with her and made her an offer; "Go wild, have whatever you want," she said. Thanks to this angel, Terry would have a wedding fully sponsored. In July 2005, just seven months after their first planned wedding, Harry and Terry got married. But another calamity was soon to knock.

Twenty-nine days later on a cold night, we couldn't sleep, so I suggested getting another duvet. But Harry said he couldn't get it as he didn't have enough strength. Strangely, I couldn't stand up either. We realized something was very wrong. Harry passed out. Moments later, Terry also passed out. At one moment, she was able to regain consciousness and pushed herself out of bed and threw up. After throwing up, she got some strength.

She remembered crawling to the phone—called the neighbor and said: "Something is wrong; Harry is not responding." That episode concluded with Terry in a hospital bed, and the doctor is giving her the shocking news; "I'm sorry, your husband did not make it."

A month early, she stood before the church alter happy getting married to the man who loved her with the Jesus kind of love–Unconditional Love. Now the man of her dreams had to be wheeled in a casket, lifeless to that same church altar. It was so unbearable for her.

She said, "I had a terrible breakdown. I felt let down by God, and I felt let down by everybody. I couldn't believe that people could be laughing, going out and just going about life. I crashed,".

Terry resolved firmly that she would never get married again, saying, "God took my husband, and the thought of ever going through such a loss again is too much for me." The pain she felt was so intense.

Thank God, one man - Tonny Gobanga kept visiting her. He encouraged her to talk about her late husband and think about the good times they shared. She didn't realize that she had fallen for the man until one time he didn't call for three days. The anger she felt because of his absence was a wake-up call that brought her to the fact that she had fallen in love with Tonny.

When Tonny proposed marriage, she told him to buy a magazine, read her story, and tell her if he still loved her. He came back and said he wanted to marry her, regardless. Three years after her first wedding, Tonny and Terry were exchanging vows. In her heart, she whispered a prayer, "Here I am again, Father, please don't let him die."

As the congregation prayed for us, I cried uncontrollably she recounted. But the wedding didn't happen without a share of misery. Tonny's family didn't want their son to marry this cursed witch of a woman.

My father-in-law refused to attend the wedding, but we went ahead anyway she said.

A year into their marriage, she felt unwell and went to the doctor, and after some examination and test, the doctor had some surprising news; he told her that she was pregnant. Yes, the stabbed womb was carrying a pregnancy.

Terry wrote a book – Crawling out of Darkness. The book details her ordeal; she aims to give people hope of rising again.

She also started an organization called Kara Olmurani. Terry works with rape survivors; that is how she calls them - not rape victims. They offer counseling and support. Now they are looking to start a halfway house for them where they can come and find their footing before going back to face the world. I think the biggest question you could ask is, 'How do you make sense out of such a life of calamity?' Shattered, broken, and suppressed dreams, How do you go beyond heartbreaking experiences of life to realize and achieve your purpose.

Above and beyond is a book of lessons on how you can recognize and overcome those setbacks on your way to your dreams. Obstacles and challenges arise from within and also from without. There are obstacles that we bring voluntarily on ourselves and their others that are inflicted on us by envious dream destroyers. Once you gain this knowledge of recognizing and overcoming these obstacles, I'll point out assurances that regardless of the frequency or magnitude of the challenges you encounter, you will arrive in the place of your purpose, that place of your destiny and dream.

I believe you are holding in your hands material that will permanently impact your journey to the destiny God ordained for you.

Many destined winners end up losses due to a lack of energy to drive on when faced with challenges.

This book will be an injection of the fuel you need to drive on no matter the hardships you encounter on your way to the top. I encourage you to settle your mind, pick a notebook for your notes, and enjoy your reading. My sincere prayer is that your life will forever be impacted by the Holy Spirit of God, who has inspired me to share my lessons on the life of Joseph through this book.

A WORD TO YOUNG PEOPLE

"You are only young once, and if you work it right, once is enough" – Joe. E. Lewis

She has gone in history as the first female president in Africa; her name is Ellen Johnson Sir-leaf. She once said that "The size of your dreams must always exceed your current capacity to achieve them. If your dreams do not scare you, they are not big enough". The younger you are, the high the propensity for big dreams. This book will help gain knowledge on how you can interpret experiences you will encounter on your way to your destiny. What do I want to achieve in this book? I want to spark a fire and passion in every young person. I want them to believe, to overcome and become. The words of Stephen R. Covey come to mind right here, "Motivation is a fire from within. If someone else tries to light that fire under you, chances are it will burn very briefly". I want to ignite a fire that already resides on the inside of you. I give you keys that will help you remain motivated consistently.

Perhaps you are a young man or lady reading this book; you are thinking to yourself saying you have many years ahead of you to take your life seriously. Before you realize it, you will be laying in the bed of regretful wishful thinking.

The days are coming when your strength fails and abilities only manifest as good tales.

Take matters into your hands, in the womb of your mind, let imagination conceive a dream for your life.

Don't settle; you have not yet started. Joseph was sold into slavery at age seventeen; he overcame sexual temptations as a youth. He rose to prominence in Egypt at the age of thirty; a wise and strategic savior in the Land. What are you or what will you be at the age of thirty? Remember Jesus too started his ministry at age thirty. Based on these examples of thirty years dream arrivals I would like to say life does not begin at forty instead it starts from the time you are born and by age thirty you must have identified and settled in your life purpose and dream.

You Are Never Too Young

Who said you should sit and watch the game of life pass you by? Must you grow old to dare? My first task is to prove to you that even as little as seven years of age, you can achieve big dreams. Let me cite some vital words for young people. Paul writes to young Timothy in 1 Timothy 4:12, "Let no man despise thy youth; but be thou an example of the believers, in word, in conversation, in charity, in spirit, in faith, in purity."

There is usually a tendency by older generations to despise younger ones. It is my conviction that young people should not relax waiting for a time when the older generation has passed for them to engage actively in life's affairs.

Both older and younger generations must find their place of purpose and call and engage fully without despising each other.

Justin Bieber believed in himself and his talent, and an opportunity appeared. He was discovered at the age of 14 and is believed to have made $110 million in those five years ever since his manager Scooter Braun stumbled across his YouTube videos.

Bieber has won several awards, including the American Music Award of the year 2010 and 2012. He has also won a Grammy Award for Best Dance Recording for the song "Where are you now." Amazingly he has also been listed by Forbes Magazine among the top ten most powerful celebrities in the world not once or twice but four times. All this he achieved before the age of 25. Let me ask you this; who said you are still young to pursue and achieve your dreams?

For the young girls and ladies out there, you are not disenfranchised because you are female. You, too, can! You probably have heard about Missy Franklin. Missy Franklin has always said that preparing to reach the highest level in her sport requires such intense dedication and focus.

Missy Franklin started trying out for the US Olympic Teams at the age of 13. With her persistence and hard work, she managed to qualify for the Olympics in 2012, when she was only 17.

By age 18 she already held four gold medals to her name. The question still stands; who said you are still young to pursue and achieve your dreams?

Mubarak Muyika is a Kenyan who founded Zagace Limited. Muyika was orphaned at the age of 10. He was excellent in school and won a scholarship to the prestigious Harvard University, but he turned that opportunity down to pursue his dream of entrepreneurship.

When he was 16, he founded Hypecentury Technologies, a web hosting company which he later sold handsomely to Wemps Telecoms and founded Zagace. The question still stands; who said you are still young to pursue and achieve your dreams?

Another phenomenon is a young man named Alain Nteff. At the age of 20, Alain had transformed his concern into a lifesaving product. Nteff was alarmed by the high death rate of newborn babies and pregnant women in his community. To answer that problem, he developed a mobile App that helps teenage mothers and health workers calculate due dates. The App also collects and sends information to women in his community. The App has had more than 500 downloads as of 2015, and it has led to a 20% increase in antenatal attendance rate for pregnant women in 15 communities. And I'm still asking the question; who said you are still young to pursue and achieve your dreams?

The Challenge

Don't just read about these inspiring stories of young people doing great things. The purpose of these stories is not to make you feel good but to challenge you to begin taking steps towards making your dream a reality.

A few years ago, you lived by the decisions of your parents but now is the time to begin living; begin to decide to make your life count. There is an evil I have seen under the sun; I have seen a tragedy; I have seen young people who are old already.

You are old if you refuse to think. Timothy Leary said, "You're only young as the last time you changed your mind."

Are you exposing yourself to the knowledge that is helping you to change your mind for you to remain relevant to your environment? If not, then you are an OLD YOUNG PERSON.

Let me briefly show you some facts with the hope of consolidating my argument that you are never too young to attempt big things.

There is no reason for you to hold back on the effort of making your dreams come true. The table below gives various names and ages of multiple personalities in the Bible who did great things in their youth. This information proves that even in the Bible, are many people who ascended to prominence at young ages.

Apart from Joseph, who became prime minister of Egypt at age thirty, the other names are of many others who became rulers while they were still kids, teenagers, and youths.

Some as young kings transformed their territories while others exhibited childish traits that ruined their kingdoms.

The list below gives thirty-five as the oldest and seven years as the youngest, giving an average age of 22.4.

Name	Age	Scripture
Joseph	30	Genesis 41:46
David	30	2 Samuel 5:4
Rehoboam	21	2 Kings 14:21
Jehoshaphat	35	1 Kings 22:42
Jehoram	32	2 Kings 8:16,17
Ahaziah	22	2 Kings 8:26
Jehoash	7	2 Kings 11:21
Amaziah	25	2 Kings 14:2
Azariah	17	2 Kings 15: 2
Jotham	25	2 Kings 15:33
Ahaz	20	2 Kings 16:2
Hezekiah	25	2 Kings 18:2
Manasseh	20	2 Kings 21:1
Amon	22	2 Kings 21:19
Josiah	8	2 Kings 22:1
Jehoahaz	23	2 Kings 23:31
Jehoiakim	25	2 Kings 23:36
Jehoiachin	18	2 Kings 24:8
Zedekiah	21	2 Kings 21:18

In this book, I want to help you the young people by giving you the knowledge you require to make your dreams come true. One thing is for sure; as you strive to achieve the purpose, you will encounter various obstacles that can cause you to give up on your dreams. My assignment in this book is to help you go above and beyond those obstacles so that you can realize your purpose.

"You are as young as your faith, as old as your doubt; as young as your self-confidence, as old as your fear; as young as your hope, as old as your despair", those words were spoken by Douglas Macarthur, telling us that there are virtues that keep an individual young or old despite their chronological age.

To be young, you need to keep alive the following virtues: FAITH, SELF-CONFIDENCE, and HOPE.

These virtues are essential to cultivate and maintain if you are going to remain young and vibrant. On the other side of the coin is another trinity: DOUBT, FEAR, and DESPAIR. The later set of virtues make you age before your time. Do you have faith in your dreams, potentials, and purpose? Do you possess self-confidence? Do you hold steadfast to hope for a better future? Or perhaps your mind is crowded with doubt and uncertainty about your dreams? Maybe you are a prisoner of fear of the unknown; why do you fear to step out and try things out. Sad if you have fallen into the ditch of despair. YOUTH ARISE!

A WORD TO OLDER PEOPLE

"Dreams are renewable no matter what our age" – Dale Turner

Let me pick up on the life of Ellen Jackson Sir-Leaf. Here is an excerpt from her book; This Child Will Be Great – Memoir of a Remarkable Life by Africa's First Woman President. "When I was just a few days old, an old man came to visit my parents, to see the new baby and to offer his good wishes, as people did both then and now in my country and everywhere. My mother brought the older man into the room where I lay kicking and cooing on the bed. As the story goes, the older man took one look at me and turned to my mother with a strange expression on his face. "Oh, Martha," he said. "This child shall be great. This child is going to lead." My mother and sister and I used to laugh whenever my mother told this story. We would laugh and laugh and laugh because, at many of the junctures in which she recalled the words of the wise older man, my life seemed anything but great.

Perhaps I was watching all my friends go off to college abroad while I stayed at home in Monrovia, trapped with an abusive husband, four young sons, and no future in view. Perhaps I was struggling to pursue my education, build my career, and divorce that husband without losing everything I had. Or maybe I was being hauled off to prison by order of my nation's president—or perhaps even plotting an escape into exile to save my life.

"Where's all this greatness that was predicted?" my mother would ask. Sometimes she laughed, sometimes she cried. Always, she prayed. "Where's that old man now?" Over the years and as the path of greatness unfolded, whenever I reflected on the prophecy of the older man, my scientific orientation Ellen Johnson Sirleaf of self-determination would clash with the Presbyterian teachings of predestination I had received. Which one, I have long wondered, is the way life is?"

Today women are proud of Ellen Johnson Sirleaf, but very few can emulate her courage. She went through an abusive marriage, a bitter divorce, imprisonment and became president after the age of sixty. She could have given up on the prophesied greatness, but she kept fighting for a better life. Like everybody, she was born for something great, but life had its challenges in stock for her. She went above and beyond them to become the first female President in Africa. "One has to look at my life story to see what I've done.

I've paid a heavy price that many people don't realize". No matter your age if you are ready, willing, and do finally pay the price, your dream can become a reality.

One thing I want you to get from this story is the fact that you, too were "Born to be a Great Child." Yours may not be to become the president of your country. Maybe you were born to touch the unloved and forsaken as Mother Teresa did. Don't let age be a limitation; go right ahead, pursue your dreams, and fulfill it.

Most people don't realize that age doesn't matter unless you let it like Satchel Paige once said that "Age is a case of mind over matter. If you don't mind, it doesn't matter".

The mistakes of youth are past; Harry and now you can with wisdom take takes to what may be a lost dream. Never make the mistake of thinking that you will live your vision through your children; they have their dreams to live. It's not too late to start, for even a day of living your dream is better than a thousand years lived without it. Why do you want to end when you have not reached the finish line. The Bible says that there is still hope; for a "living dog is better than a dead lion." Don't resign from life while you are still living. Why do you want to be taken off life's game and to be thrown in the trash six feet deep when you have not yet expired? There are great things to be achieved before you reach your expiry date. Dare to dream again! Don't lose heart my elder; you've got a lot going for you. There is an exciting adage which says, "The early bird may get the worm, but the second mouse gets the cheese." Instead of seeing yourself as the late bird who finds no warm, see yourself as the second mouse who wins the ultimate price – the cheese. You could have missed your opportunities early in life, but you can win by having a second look at your mistakes.

Live At Any Age

"Too many people, when they get old, think that they have to live by the calendar" – John Glenn.

Talk of daring, John Glenn did just that. When most old-timers think the fascination of flying in space is something for the youth, Glenn has gone into history as the oldest man to fly in space. As the oldest person to board a U.S. Space Shuttle at age 77, Senator John Glenn exemplified the view that we shouldn't let age define or limit us.

Instead of sitting and rocking in an armchair feeling miserable about life, Glenn has shown the world that one should not let age be a hindrance to a life of energetic pursuits. The point is that the calendar is a useful way to let you know the date, but if you let yourself be hemmed in by your chronological age, you may lock yourself out of potentially valuable opportunities. Dare to dream and dare to go after your dream no matter your age.

"How old would you be if you didn't know how old you were" – Satchel Paige

Satchel Paige like John Glenn has also gone into history for being the oldest in his field of endeavor. Paige was celebrated as a trailblazer baseball pitcher. On his 42nd birthday, he became the oldest player to debut in the major leagues, as well as the first

Negro league pitcher in the American League. As though trying to secure his record, at age fifty-nine he enshrined his name in history as the oldest pitcher in a baseball league.

> *"Those who think they have no time for bodily exercise will sooner or later have to find time for illness" – Edward Stanley (1826-1893)*

When your mind is convinced that you are past the age for physical exercise, then your body will automatically begin to shut down. Edward Stanley was a British statesman who advocated for the importance of good health through regular physical activity. Often as people age, they tend to grow a bag of medicines of all sorts. Daily physical activity can keep away that bag of medicine for a long while.

Engage in activities that will rejuvenate and revitalize your youthful spirit.

"Aging is not lost youth but a new stage of opportunity and strength" – Betty Friedan (1921-2006)

In her book "The Fountain of age," Betty Friedan wrote, "Let's redefine later life as a time of growth instead of inevitable decline." Stop allowing age to limit your dreams. Yes, you got to be realistic about your dreams but never fear to dream big. Often, aging populations are so obsessed with age that they stop living. Despite your age, I want to encourage you by saying that you've got to break out of the mindset that makes you think of your age first and your identity second. You are here and alive for a purpose. Focus on that purpose and start living. Your goal is who you are, not your age.

"Anyone who stops learning is old, whether at twenty or eighty. Anyone who keeps learning stays young. The greatest thing in life is to keep your mind young" – Henry Ford

Never Stop Learning

In conclusion, here is a key to igniting your dreams and keeping them alive. Yes, because of old age you've got the experience, but that is not a certificate of graduation from the school of life. The world is continuously changing, and you can't remain behind.

George Sand once said that "Try to keep your soul young and quivering right up to old age," informing us that you can and must strive to keep mind, will, and passion alive through deliberate action. Learning helps you to keep stirring the spirit of youth even in old age. Dive into the world of science and technology don't be trapped in the BBC (Born Before Computer) mentality. Some opportunities can accord you the chance to live your life with a sense of satisfaction, not regret. NEVER STOP LEARNING; that is the key to saying young no matter your age.

It's never too late to work out your dreams. Don't apologize for the way you lived in the past, and you can do something about your tomorrow. You can finish well.

I wish you the best of success. Read on!

A hero is an ordinary individual who finds the strength to persevere and endure in spite of

overwhelming obstacles – Christopher Reeve

CHAPTER ONE

THE DREAMER'S DILEMMA

"It is difficult to say what is possible, for the dream of yesterday is the hope of today and the reality of tomorrow" – Robert H. Goddard

Robert H. Goddard describes in unambiguous terms what the bible character Joseph went through. Joseph dreamed that one day he would be exalted above his brethren and that his father and mother too would 'kneel' down before him. His father said "impossible," while his brothers picked an issue with him. The world of dreams is a world of infinite possibility. To many people, dreams are just meaningless mind indulgencies that have no significance in the real world. In the world of dreams and ideas, all things are possible; birds can fly backward, man can outrun the cheetah, and the lion can eat grass.

In the world of dreams, even the beaten become mighty

men; conquering new frontiers and establishing dynasties.

It is a world of grave dangers, and yet still, a paradise of joyous victories, like Eleanor Roosevelt said:

"The future belongs to those who believe in the beauty of the dream."

Believing in your dreams gives you hope in the present, thus keeping you motivated so that you can move on with persistence to realize your dreams despite the odds.

In the recess of sound sleep, men dream only to awake to a reality far different from their dreams, yet others with their eyes fully awake dream in the depth of imagination. It is those dreams in your imagination that count. I'm sure you might have felt that frustration or the relief that comes with the realization that "it was just a dream." Wither awake or in a deep sleep; all individuals dream. In this discourse, I will be using the terms dream and imagination rather liberally as being interchangeable.

The idea is that wither it happens in sleep or active conscious thinking, a dream is a vision, aspiration, pursuit, or plan whose realization or attainment promises individual satisfaction and fulfillment. Here is something important to remember; "Those who dream by day are cognizant of many things which escape those who dream only by night." Edgar Allen Poe makes a vital point in the above quote. A person who dreams in awake in the workshop of imagination is aware of many factors – both supporting and opposing. Dreaming awake helps you remain in control of your dreams

What Is Your Dream?

Many people don't see themselves as having a dream in their lives.

Well, if you are one of those people then take time to ponder on what Emma Goldman said: "When we can't dream any longer we die."

You might be that person as you read this book, that is saying, "I don't have a dream."

The starting point is for you to answer a fundamental question, what are dreams? Let me give some light on what dreams are. First of all, I want you to know that in simple terms, dreams are mental projections of the desired future. Every individual is striving to be better than their present. No matter how well accomplished a person is, there is still a propensity for a betterment. For most people, the attainment of a set goal gives birth to another target. Other people refer to their dreams as a personal vision. A dream is a summary of what you want to do or hope to be in life. "God has placed within each person a vision that is designed to give purpose and meaning to life" – Dr. Myles Munroe.

Your dream is that intense desire in your heart; the desire for self-fulfillment by expressing your true self.

That dream is not to be sort outside 'YOU' but is to be found by looking into yourself.

The blunt truth is that by focusing on self, you discover that dream. As mentioned above, dreams may come to you in the recess of sound sleep or the realm of imagination. You too have a dream. And you will not find satisfaction and fulfillment in life till you discover that dream and begin to take steps to its realization.

It is beyond the scope of this book to show how to discover dreams. I would recommend two books that have helped me in my dream discovery journey, "THE PRINCIPLES AND POWER OF VISION" by Dr. Myles Munroe as good reading for vision discovery and the other book is by my mentor Dr. Sunday Adelaja's 'WHO AM I, WHY AM I HERE.'

Dreams Have Wings; They Fly Away

Allow me to familiarize you with the ordeal of a Bible character called Job. As though losing his children and all his wealth was not enough, Job's affliction was multiplied by a visit from his best friends. Instead of sympathizing and empathizing with him, they condemned him and treated him as a sinner. They pointed to his misfortune as resulting from his disobedience to God. Anyhow, beyond their disheartening comments one of Job's friends gives a bright characteristic of dreams, he says, "He shall fly away as a dream, and shall not be found: yea, he shall be chased away as a vision of the night" Job 20:8.

It's important to understand that dreams can fly away from consciousness; therefore, the need to cage them. Wither they be dreams of sleep or imagination dreams, they all have this ability. This ability of dreams shows a behavior as if they are banished from an individual's conscious mind by some force.

You may even try hard to remember them, but they are nowhere to be found, lost in nothingness. Because people don't know how to cage (retain) their dreams, they end up frustrated once their dreams fly away.

It is a sad reality; there are many lost dreams out there existing in the realm of nothingness. Dreams that could have changed families and transformed societies have been forgotten and lost, oh what a shame many dreams are not recalled.

It happened to King Nebuchadnezzar, in Daniel 2:5, "The king answered and said to the Chaldeans, The thing is gone from me…"

The King had forgotten the dreams he had, but these dreams left an impression on his mind and emotions so much so that he had to demand the wise men of Babylon to tell him what he dreamt. The dreams escaped his consciousness. This is the first challenge that men face; the loss of dreams from consciousness. You may have a dream in the form of an idea, but because of a lack of knowledge on how to cage it, you end up losing it. Most times, people tend to lose sight of their passions and dreams. Like Nebuchadnezzar, many people fail to remember their dreams.

There is some good news for you; please continue reading. I have given helpful tips to teach you how to cage your dreams.

"Nothing happens unless first a dream" – *Carl Sandburg*

Did you know that the purest of dreams are dreams of children? When children dream they don't think of the failing economy, the poverty or wealth of their parents.

They don't limit their dreams to education or country of residence. Children dream big. Sad to say that as they grow up and see or experience the harsh conditions of the world around them, they tend to lose sight of their dreams.

Robert Kiyosaki says, "People who dream small dreams continue to live as small people." Usually, people start as young children with big dreams and aspiration, but those big dreams begin to reduce day by day. By the time one is in their late teens, they have settled for the status quo.

I want to introduce to you three ways in which you can cage your dreams so that they don't elude you. Caging your dream will ensure that no matter the obstacles you face, your dream will not be lost.

> *"Awakening, I immediately wrote it down*
> *on a piece of paper" – Dmitri Mendeleev*

Caging Your Dream

Having seen the nature of dreams in that, they have the ability to fly away, let us discover how you can overcome this tragedy of dream banishment? I recommend three practices or habits of ensuring every dream of yours is retained. Simple and easy they may seem; these points of dream retention are crucial for you to master and apply. Wither dreams of the night sleep or imagination of the fully awake mind; these points will prove helpful in your quest to cage your dreams.

1.   **Meditate**: Take serious thought about your dream. If it occurs to you in the night, take a few moments to think

about it thoroughly. You are identifying the key players or main characters in your dream. Recognize the central theme of the dream and ponder on the various scenes. If the dream occurs in the realm of imagination still take some time to be in a quiet place to do the same; identify critical players, themes, scenes, etc. This meditation helps to retain your dream for a while but should never be the ending point of your efforts in dream retention.

2.   **Share**: Most people out there are terrified of sharing their dreams for fear of ridicule and the possibility of their dreams being hijacked. There is a right audience for you to share your dreams with. And indeed, there is a wrong audience. No one can do what you were born to do the way you would do it. I believe a dream is intrinsic to the dreamer. Dismiss the fear of sharing your dreams with others. A desire not shared is a dream limited. Sharing your dream allows its growth; when a dream is subject to a second opinion, more light shines on it, and any overlooked areas are made visible. In a later chapter, I discuss the caution to be taken in dream sharing to avoid destructive criticism.

3.   **Document**: The most effective way to retain your dream is by writing it down. "Write the revelation and make it plain on tablets so that a herald may run with it. For

the revelation awaits an appointed time; it speaks of the end and will not prove false. Though it lingers, wait for it, it will certainly come and will not delay..." Habakkuk 2:2 – 4. It is often said that "The pen is the tongue of the mind." Lack of dream documentation gives birth to a lack of focus. The point is that a dream document will instill a high level of discipline required to bring the dream into reality. It will act as a map or campus to ensure you stay on course. Even the most powerful of minds will not retain all the information it encounters hence the need for a tangible record. In a time of meditation, you can take the written down dream and subject it to further thought and scrutiny. Please write your dream.

It is important to note that the best practice is for you to meditate and document your dreams in one activity. As you think deeply about your dream, please endeavor to write down your thoughts.

Write out:

1.   The theme of your dream

2.   The characters in your dream

3.   The scenes of your dream

4.   The feelings or emotions in your dreams

5.   The challenges in your dreams

This is what I do; if an idea happens to wander through my

mind, I immediately write it down. Using modern gadgets, I use my phone to store a note of the idea. I always sleep with a pen and paper nearby. If a night dream appears to be of significance; I wake up to write it down. I don't know about you, but for me, I have mastered the discipline of waking up no matter how deep in sleep I could be. Well, that works for me. You too, have got to find what works for you. But whatever you do please endeavor to document your dreams and ideas the very moment they occur.

Reality Of Dreams

Dreams are realities even when they are forgotten or unrealized. A lost or unrealized dream will always leave its impressions on the mind and emotions of the dreamer. So is a dream unfulfilled? "…, and my spirit was troubled to know the dream". Daniel 2:3b.

King Nebuchadnezzar woke from his sleep a troubled man. He knew the source of his trouble was the dream he had even though it was gone from him. We can see from this story that dreams are such mental realities that they can stress the dreamer if lost or not worked out into physical or tangible reality.

There is a famous Japanese proverb that says, "Vision without action is a daydream and action without vision is a nightmare." Many people live lives that are a nightmare because they lack a dream or a vision. And still, there are many out there who for the lack of action have reduced their dreams to mere daydreams. It is frustrating and emotionally draining. When you have a dream, and you can't muster the courage to pursue it, the dream will end up frustrating you. It will so bother you that it will affect your whole life. It's better not to have a dream than to have one and not take any deliberate step towards its realization.

"A plan is a bridge to your dreams. Your job is to make the plan or bridge real so that your dreams will become a reality. If all you do is stand on the side of the bank and dream of the other side, your dreams will forever be just dreams. First, make your plans real, and then your dreams will come true". The words were spoken by Robert Kiyosaki, giving us great insights. Dreams require plans, or they will forever remain dreams. Dreams only become useful when they are implemented in physical reality. You have to make your dream come true. It won't happen accidentally but through deliberate planning and action.

Daydreaming

Daydreams are "a series of pleasant thoughts that distract one's attention from the present.

This practice of daydreaming has been condemned by many as a wasteful preoccupation. But I would like to forward my thoughts on daydreaming. Firstly we need to appreciate that we must live in the present but also think in futuristic terms. Don't be absent-minded but also don't be afraid to let your mind visit the future through the power of imagination. If your thinking is in the present, you will always live in the past. The ability to change the present lies in futuristic thinking and not present thinking itself.

It is essential to do some time traveling; go into your tomorrow with your imagination and then come into the present to implement strategies that will take your 'present' to the future your mind has visited. With your imagination, you can visit the future, see what it is made of and come into the present to take the steps to that future.

Let me share with you a story that changed Chemistry and our world. Psychologists suggest that what happens during night visions (dreams) is organizing and consolidating the ideas, images, and bits of information that occupy our waking hours.

Well, Dmitry experience seems to vindicate the claim. It is said that Dmitry Mendeleyev was on a three-day work bender when he finally gave in for a few minutes of shut-eye.

Instead of falling asleep under the power of a tired mind like most sleep-deprived people, Mendeleyev dreamt of an arrangement of elements that would change modern chemistry forever. He then popped up about 20 minutes later to record it.

He said that "I saw in a dream a table where all the elements fell into place as required. Awakening, I immediately wrote it down on a piece of paper". Before the breakthrough, he said, "It's all formed in my head, but I can't express it."

It was only when he traveled into his head under the spell of sleep's uninhibited state that he was able to see disjointed bits fell into a pattern and the broader idea expressed itself.

> *"An incredibly good feeling, a lesson for*
> *all dreamers ... that you can have a dream*
> *and it can come true" – Tim Berners Lee*

Let's dive a little more into the issue of daydreaming.

More than fifty years ago, pioneering research led by Yale's Jerome L. Singer established that daydreaming is a widespread and regular aspect of human experience. In his study, Singer found that significant society classifications consist of "happy daydreamers"— these are people who enjoy vivid imagery and fantasy. They engage in daydreaming as an exercise for plotting out their future. These daydreamers "simply value and enjoy their private experiences, are willing to risk wasting a certain amount of time on them, but also can use them for effective planning and self-amusement during periods of monotonous task activity or boredom," Singer reported. He called this "positive-constructive daydreaming." There are three main categories of daydreams: these are Poor Attention Control, Guilty-dysphoric, and Positive-constructive daydreaming. Let me explain a little further on these forms.

The first style of daydreams is called "poor attention control." This form is usually characterized by easy distractibility and difficulty concentrating on either the external environment or an ongoing train of thought. People with this style do not report elaborate daydreams and score low in conscientiousness.

The second style of daydreaming is called "Guilty-dysphoric" daydreaming. This form of daydreaming features unpleasant emotions such as anxiety, guilt, fear of failure, and obsessive, hostile and aggressive fantasies about others. Such daydreamers are highly illogical. And lastly, there is "positive-constructive" daydreaming. It is associated with openness to experience and reflecting a drive to explore ideas, imagination, feelings, and sensations.

The merits hold that openness to experience is linked to

many indicators of psychological health, including happiness, positive emotions, and high quality of life.

Given these three forms or styles of daydreaming, we should avoid the trap of condemning all forms of daydreaming. The first two are counterproductive, but the third is very important and should be embraced.

Others call it "futuristic thinking," but whatever you call it, daydreaming is an essential practice of successful people. It is a form of time travel. So release your mind and let it take you to the places you've never been to before. Unleash your mental potential through daydreaming.

Dream Vanities

"For in the multitude of dreams and many words, there are also divers vanities: but fear thou, God." Ecclesiastes 5:7. The danger here being given is that one should never cast aside the fear of God just because we have a dream.

Dream indulgencies apart from practical Godly wisdom is all vanity. Dr. Sunday Adelaja says, "When you come to know God personally, and He becomes your close friend, you will live an easy and fulfilled life." What is implied here is not a challenge-free life but peace and serenity amid challenge – only God can offer such serenity. Remember, it's only God who can do above your imagination (see Ephesians 3:20). In partnership with God, man's impossibilities become possibilities.

Dear friend, remember the fear of God is never to leave your heart for it is the starting point of all wisdom needed for dream realization.

In conclusion, having looked at basic dream principles, it is vital to keep these principles in mind as we study the life of Joseph.

The dilemma of dreamers is that dreams speak of the future, but the voice is heard in the present, surrounded by different circumstances and vivid limitations.

"It shall even be as when a hungry man dreameth, and, behold, he eateth; but he awaketh, and his soul is empty: or as when a thirsty man dreameth, and, behold, he drinketh; but he awaketh, and, behold, he is faint, and his soul hath appetite:" Isaiah 29:8a.

Imagine the frustrations of such a dreamer who dreams having a delicious meal and only to wake up hungry or another person who dreams of an electronic breakthrough invention and wakes up to the fact that he does not know electronics.

The point the scripture is giving us here is that it is frustrating to have a dream and live in a reality that is so at variance from the dream.

This dilemma has kept many people from driving forward

to realizing their dreams. Above and Beyond strives to help you get a right perspective on life circumstances so that nothing that happens to you extinguishes the energy needed to drive you to your dream.

What better example to look at other than the life of Joseph: He dreamt, he shared, got rejected and sold, he was enslaved, imprisoned, and disappointed and finally he reached his dream destination.

There are vital lessons to be learned from this gallant patriarch. In Above and Beyond these lessons are explored and vividly made bare for you to relate to your life for a meaningful life application.

> *No matter the challenges or obstacles to*
> *your dreams, you have what it takes to go*
> *Above and Beyond to reach your dreams.*

CHAPTER TWO

YOUR FAMILY AND YOUR DREAM

"The family is the essential presence – the thing that never leaves you, even if you find you have to leave it" – Bill Buford

The first unit of society God made was the family, which started with Adam and Eve, who later birthed Cain and Abel his brother. Thus the first family was constituted. Many people out there wish they could have been born in this or that family, in one country or continent, and unfortunately, they blame God for their present family and country of birth. Bill Buford expresses an important point – "The family is the essential presence – thee thing that never leaves you, even if you find you have to leave it." The family is essential to our development; it is the vital unit that fosters healthy social, emotional and even financial growth.

I am reminded of a story of a kindergartener who was always picked to and from school by a hired taxi. One day as the child was being driven home, he started singing, "If my father was a king my mother would be a queen, and I'd be a prince."

The taxi driver then hushed the child. Children being children; the child continued singing, this time adding another line to his lyrics, "If my father were a king, my mother would be a queen, and I'd be a prince. If my father were the president, my mother would be the first lady, and I'd be the first son." In an angry tone, the driver interjected and asked, "What if your father was a robber, what would your mother be and what would you be?" And without any hesitation, the child responded, "If my father were a robber, my mother would be a prostitute, and I'd be a taxi driver."

Born to an interracial couple Jerome and Judith, living in the inner-city neighborhood Halle Berry went through a childhood that could have crushed her spirit and potential. In the early 1970s, Jerome Berry abandoned his wife and two children, after which Judith moved her family to the predominantly white Cleveland suburb of Bedford.

Some life changes, such as changing cities or schools, are never easy most, especially for children. While in Bedford

Halle Berry attended a nearly all-white public school, and as a result, was subjected to discrimination at an early age. When others suffer from low self-esteem due to racial discrimination, Halle Berry's first bouts with racism greatly influenced her desire to excel.

Eleanor Roosevelt once said, "You gain strength, courage, and confidence by every experience in which you really stop to look fear in the face. You must do the thing you think you cannot do".

In the face of racial discrimination, Berry did just that, she remained forceful and resolute, never going into a corner and allow the labeling of others to define her life and what she could do.

Throughout high school, she remained determined and participated in a dizzying array of extracurricular activities, holding positions of a newspaper editor, class president, and head cheerleader.

Fast-forward beyond high school Berry attended Cleveland's Cuyahoga Community College for a short time, where she studied broadcast journalism. However, Berry abandoned her idea of a career in news reporting before receiving her degree, choosing to wholeheartedly devote her time to a career in entertainment. Just follow her career trail; you will end up with a lot of honors, and success on every turn.

Halle Berry now has an Oscar and is one of the most popular actresses in Hollywood, but the lesson we can see is that she went through her struggles as well before making it big. There is an African proverb which says, "Smooth seas do not make skillful sailors." Even pursuing her passion was not a smooth sail. At the start of her acting career, she first moved to Chicago staying at a homeless shelter on and off. She ran out of money after making a move to Chicago, and her mother could not give her any money saying that she would be making her daughter stronger; tough love right there.

Halle Berry said that it did make her stronger and further made her want success more than ever. Berry said that she learned how to live through any situation, whether she had to live at a homeless shelter or live very close to the poverty line.

These experiences and lessons made her into a person that always makes sure that she gets what she wants and will stop at nothing to succeed. In the light of this story, if your father abandoned you what would your mother be and what would you be?"

If your father was a drunk, what would your mother be and what would you be?" If your father was a laborer, what would your mother be and what would you be?" And what if your father was a robber? "If my father were a robber, my mother would be a prostitute, and I'd be a taxi driver." Well, that is the answer only a child can give.

 Do you ever wish you were a millionaire's son or the president's daughter or probably a high school teacher's child? Indeed many are the thoughts that race in the minds of many people concerning their family and country of birth; many people desire to relocate, believing that a better and satisfying life awaits them over the shore.

A better life is not waiting for you overseas but 'oversees.' The point is that a better life lays in you seeing better than you are presenting seeing.

It is saddening that there are people in their forties, fifties still trapped in wishful thinking, wishing they had a good father and instead of concentrating on being the good father to their children, they make wrecks of their own lives; what a tragedy.

Thousands have crossed seas and oceans in search of the place of their dreams, thank God others have made it, and yet others have ended up destitute on foreign soil.

We blame mother, father, brother, sister, the state governor, president but never take time to look at what God has to say about it all. I want to highlight from the onset that family has been, still is and will always be a cardinal component in the plan of God for your life.

The first government God create was the family, which he blessed and gave dominion over the earth, to take care of it, to rule and to subdue it. From this family, God desired that all humanity should proceed, having the care and protection required to grow up and continue populating the earth and fulfilling God's mandate. It is for this reason that God created all humanity in one man Adam; he created He them; male and female. "So God created man in his image, in the image of God created He him; male and female created He them." Genesis 1:27. He created them with the ability to propagate seed after their nature, and so in Adam and Eve, God created Cain, Abel, Seth…, You and Me. The enemy succeeded in removing the first family from the presence of his Creator and all hell broke loose.

If you look at Joseph's family, even without the scrutiny of the scriptures, you see trouble spelled in every detail.

Father Jacob, mother Rachel, step mum Leah, and eleven brothers not all from the same woman for a fact, it was a complicated family. Jealous, competition, quarrying, fighting, backbiting, and many other vices characterized this family.

In the rational analysis, you may be led to conclude that no right, significant individual would rise from such a family to rule the vast land of Egypt of that day. Joseph's brothers, who should have shown love and protection turned to be dangerous wolves and preyed on him.

The scars of family betrayal are tough to overcome; the rape of a young girl by an uncle without the healing of God can leave a damaging scar. The dreams of your life may have been poisoned with the cruelty of loved ones, and it has become hard to muster the strength to move on. Maybe you have undergone a painful divorce, and you don't see yourself rebuilding your dreams apart from your lost marriage partner. Perhaps it might have been the verbal abuse you suffered from parents and guardians that called you a 'nothing.' All these and many various painful experiences at the hand of the family tend to limit many people in the pursuit of their dreams if they fail to make sense out of them.

"It is easier to build strong children than to repair broken men" – Frederick Douglass

Concepts Of The Ideal Family

For this section, I want to draw thoughts from an article by Robert Taibbi titled "The Ideal Family: How Do You Stack

Up? – A quick family assessment guide. Robert gives various family structures; four structures present an unhealthy family, then he shows how an ideal family is structured.

We shall look at these five family structures now: we shall adopt the diagrams Robert uses to illustrate the structures. Let P stand for parents, C for children, the Solid line between Ps and Cs for hierarchy.

The solid line connecting the two parents means that the parents are emotionally connected and on the same page about parenting. The solid line connecting children means even though there is sibling rivalry, the kids get along and care about each other. Keep these connections in mind.

> *"A child who is allowed to be disrespectful*
> *to his parents will not have true respect for*
> *anyone" – Bill Graham*

1.   **Child in Control, parents feel like Victims:** This is the worst structure of the family. A child is in control, and this usually the eldest child. The child mostly runs the family; he/she acts up and pretty much does what he/she wants. The parents feel like the victims of his/her demands and emotions. In such a case, a child grows up with no sense of authority in his life and as such may turn out a wreck. Did you grow up in this kind of family? Was it you

or one of your siblings who was running the show? The diagram of this structure looks as shown below:

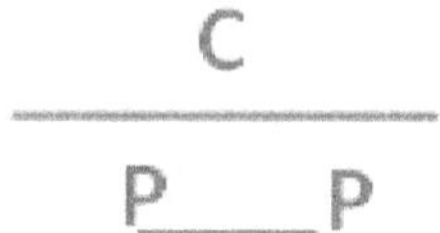

***"Each day of our lives we make deposits in the memory banks of our children"* –**

Charles R. Swindoll

2.   **Isolated parent, other parent uses children as support**: In this structure, the parents are not emotionally connected. The isolated parent doesn't feel part of the family. He/she may be having an affair or absent because of being a workaholic or some form of addiction. The other parent who mostly is left feeling lonely tends to find consolation and support from the children, and usually the eldest child. Thus the child is parentified. Parentified children tend to assume adulthood responsibility before their full maturity and may in later years suffer from regression (an individual's personality reverts to an earlier stage of development). The lonely parent may cultivate in the parentified child feelings of resentment and anger towards the isolated parent. The diagram of this structure looks as shown below:

P | P____C

3.   **Hierarchy, other parent united with children as victims**: Here, one parent is the "head of the house" and solely runs the show. The other parent has slipped to the level of the children. This kind of family is reasonably common in addictive or abusive families. The parent who has slipped down feels victimized and may periodically threaten divorce but is persuaded to be the dominant parent promising to play it nice. The downgraded parent usually becomes the ring-leader of the children and can influence them to revolt against the dominant parent. This situation can put the children in a very awkward position, sometimes having to take sides even if it is just for a while to please one parent. The diagram of this structure looks as shown below:

P
____

P____C

4.   **Hierarchy, parents disagree, children confused/testing and splitting**: Here, both parents are

above the children but not united. Regarding parenting, they are not on the same page. One may be hard while the other easy on the children. In such a scenario, the kids tend to be confused. Sibling rivalry is egregious because children tend to pick sides and alienate each other. The parents fuel this alienation by disagreeing and being on different pages and sometimes don't even realize the negative impact this has on the children. The diagram of this structure looks as shown below:

$$P \text{------} P$$

$$\overline{}$$

$$C \text{---} C \text{---} C$$

Many of you reading this book may have been raised in any of these families I have highlighted above. Maybe you assume adult responsibility early in life, perhaps you grew a lot of bitterness towards an isolated parent and you still struggle with that today. Many of us have grown up in dysfunctional families, and we do things that jeopardize our purpose and destiny without knowing. As a result of such experiences, you may have deficiencies in character, and that might hamper your chance of fulfilling your destiny. One thing you can do when you have your own family is to cultivate the principles of an ideal family. So what does the structure of an ideal family look like?

Joseph too lived in a dysfunctional family. You see, the father favoring Joseph over other children. You see, the eldest taking responsibility for the family business. Joseph was exposed continuously to the rivalry between his two mothers; Rachael and Leah. Joseph had a deficiency that I will highlight later on in this book; he failed to mind his own business. It was the family structure that sponsored and encouraged the weakness of badmouthing his brothers. What then is the ideal family?

5.   **Hierarchy, Parents United, both involved with children**: In this situation, parents are over the children and are emotionally connected, standing on the same page regarding parenting. Parents stand together on parenting standards children are not confused or tempted to play one parent against the other. In this scenario, the children feel less anxious and safe, knowing that both parents are in charge rather than one of them. This represents an ideal family. The diagram of this structure looks as shown below:

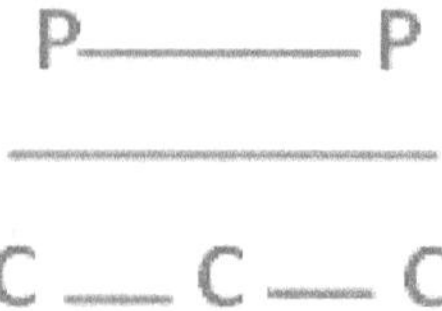

***"At the end of the day, the most
overwhelming key to a child's success is
the positive involvement of parents" –
Jane D. Hull***

There is Good News for You

Now, you may be asking what the good news is in all this.
Well, God created another family through his son Jesus
Christ. The Love you did not know in your biological
family God has provided through the spiritual family. The
encouragement to replace and wipe away the years of
discouragement, disappointment, and verbal abuse you
could have been subjected to is now sufficient for you in
Christ Jesus our Lord. Thank God for both your biological
and spiritual family because no matter the trouble you
suffered, you will arrive safely in the place of your dreams.

If you are a born-again Christian, then you have cause to
rejoice in the Lord for your new-found family through
which you will find all the vitamins and nourishment you
need on your journey to your dreams. For those of different
faiths who may not understand the concept of the Christian
family.

Many avenues are there for your nourishment. One such channel is mentorship. If your parents are not able to stand as role models and inspire you, you can look to someone who can adopt you in a mentorship relationship.

> *"There are illegitimate parents, but I don't believe there are any illegitimate children"*
> *– Rick Warren*

To your parents, you might have been a biological accident, but to God, you are no accident at all. Your parents are not accidents in your life; God planned you to be in that family. You might be in a dysfunctional family; absent father, alcoholic mother, and drug-abusing siblings. What you need is the love, care, and protection which God has provided through the spiritual family.

If you will surrender your life to Jesus Christ and let him take over, your life will have a new dawn and perspective on various issues of life. And you will find the strength to move on no matter the hurdles you encounter in your journey. Always remember this; perspective is everything. The story of Joseph and many others in the Bible, like that of Job, serve to give you and me a new perspective on life's journey.

We should appreciate these heroes of the faith like Joseph, for by their faithfulness to God, we have valuable lessons for our admonition, strengthening, and encouragement.

Having recognized the two families, I would like to point out to you the fact that in Christ Jesus, you have a super DNA. Biologically you might have inherited what others may term as unpopular genes for success and completion.

Maybe when you look closely at your family, no one has accomplished anything worthwhile. You are afraid that you are just going to end up like your father, grandfather, etc. For sure if the only family you are born into is that biological family then it's likely you will end up like the rest of your family, remember you carry their hereditary instructions.

In Christ, God has provided a new set of hereditary instructions for those born to his family for their survival, growth, and reproduction. If you can only realize that in Christ, you are a new man, a man of capabilities for possibilities, you will run to accomplish every dream God has planted in you.

So there is no need for you to shade any more tears for the lost love and care, there is plenty of supply in your new family.

Oh what joy to belong to a family of winners, you belong to that tribe of the conquering Lion of Judah.

Your biological family limitation should no longer be a

reality to you because Christ Jesus has become your reality. Keep on reading, and I will show you how you can go above and beyond those family limitations.

You can go Above and Beyond your Family Limitation

"We never know the love of a parent till we become parents ourselves" – Henry Ward Beecher

CHAPTER THREE

THE ROAD TO YOUR DREAM

"The Knowledge Of The Laws Of Life Makes Life Predictable." – Sunday Adelaja

Having looked at how family experience can impact our journey to our purpose, we need to realize that the negatives or positives in our families should never be seen as the ultimate limitations of our destinies. We all have a road to travel; there is a journey to embark on. It is that journey that ultimately sharps the outcome of our destiny. To be more precise – it is our response to the things we encounter on the journey that sharps our future. In this chapter, we are going to look at the different types of journeys or paths that lay before us. The biggest problem most people face is not the lack of a dream but the knowledge and wisdom to make it happen. When you get a glimpse of the future that awaits you, it excites every atom of your being; you wish you could reach it tomorrow.

Between today and your dream lays a journey. There are several ways of getting to your dreamland, and as such, I would like to highlight these ways to contextualize the story of Joseph.

Life Can Be Predictable.

You don't have to leave your life by chance; you can take control and determine the outcome of your life by following the laws that govern life. This section will shade more light on how you can ensure that your dreams become realities. Joseph's story will help us learn critical life lessons. Understanding this section is the key to appreciating the events that unfold in the life of this young King called Joseph. You must know that life's journey takes three popular routes. These are; the normal route, the shortcut route, and the divine route. Let's discuss them in details:

From the normal alphabetical order, you get only one word – NO. If you are normal don't expect much from life!

The Normal Route

Life may appear to be as simple as A, B, C, But my dear get real, life can be complicated. The A, B, C. is the normal alphabet. The question I can ask you is; from the normal order of the alphabet, how many words can you come up with?

I did try to make up several words from the normal alphabetical order, and I could only come up with one word: "NO." The normal is good, but it does not give you enough training to handle the success at the place of your dreams. Come to think of it, the people that have made a difference are those who dared to differ from the normal.

A normal route to your destiny gives you few opportunities to think and do things outside the norm. The normal route brings you into your dreamland half-baked.

> *"Playing things too safe is the most*
> *popular way to fail." – Elliot Smith*

One thing is sure, normal is comfortable, and it dismisses any demands outside the familiar territories. Normal is acceptable; it offers a sense of safety and control over one's life yet inhibiting the rich potentials vested within an individual. Thus many end up trading greatness of potential exploration for a little sense of security. Play it safe is the popular encouragement which is an admonishment to stick to the normal.

One thing I love about men and women of the Bible is that their lives were extraordinary (extra-normal).

The mighty Samson, ruddy David, discerning Daniel, the enigma Apostle Paul, these are just a few of the ordinary men who lived extraordinarily.

They lived the normal abnormally. If your story is out of the normal, no need to give excuses but instead give praises. God uses normal people to do the above normal things through normal means.

Your journey to dreamland will be characterized by various unusual happenings. It should not lead you to despair, rejoice! For destiny, the journey is never a normal straight path. There are mountains to climb, valleys to endure and rivers to cross. Joyce Meyer says, "So now, I exhort you with this truth; don't spend all your life playing it safe! Safety is very comfortable, but it may be keeping you from God's perfect plan for your life".

The Shortcut Route

A shortcut is an act of impatience and desperation. Never be in a hurry to make things happen that God is not making happen. Abraham was destined to be a father of many nations by his wife, Sarah. He consented to Sarah's suggestion of fulfilling God's promise to them through a servant girl named Hagar. Ishmael was the result, and the boy proved to be a problem to them, and they had to send Hagar out together with her son Ishmael, (see Genesis 16: 1–3).

The legendary Michael Jordan said, "Be true to the game

because the game will be true to you. If you try to shortcut the game, then the game will shortcut you. If you put forth the effort, good things will be bestowed upon you. That's true about the game, and in some ways, that's true about life too,"The point is that life will shortcut you if you decided to take shortcuts.

Shortcuts are the easiest and sometimes the cheapest ways to reaching an intended goal. The journey to your dreamland will cost you a lot of resources. You must be willing to pay that price if you are to reach your dreamland legitimately. The Lord Jesus was to die on the cross for the salvation of humanity, and that cross was an unavoidable necessity.

Shortcuts entail avoidance of due process to an outcome.

Many a time the process to the outcome is the price you have to pay, never forget that. Many people know what it takes to be successful, but they are never willing to pay the price; hence, they remain dreaming all their lives, what a tragedy.

The Divine Route

The normal is the route men prefer, the shortcut is the route the enemy would have you take, but there is another way; the way of God. God has the best way to take you to your dreamland, and when you reach it, you will be persevered in that land and enjoy a sustained lifelong reign.

The divine route extracts all ills that would otherwise be carried to that land of your dream. All hidden character foils are exposed to provide a learning opportunity.

You may never know what hides deep in your core until you are subjected to a destiny journey via the divine route.

Never dread the dealings of God in regard to the path He allows for your life; you will come out refined. The journey is the refiner's fire meant to burn out all the impurities that hide the gold that you are. "Strength does not come from winning. Your struggles develop your strength. When you go through hardships and decide not to surrender, that is strength"—Arnold Schwarzenegger

Most intriguing is the journey of Joseph from the time of his dreaming to its actualization. There are stops or pauses in the journey, but they all have a role in character refining. The only place where you get stack is the land of your dream but if you have not arrived at the dream of your life, press on. You can become, and by God's providence, you will become the man or woman in your dreams.

Pausing a film does not entail its end; therefore look forward to more action ahead. The movie of your life has not yet ended, it may be on pause but thank God for the play button; and our earnest prayer should be something like, "Oh Lord, play on, the movie of my life."

Oh Dreamer, never despair, the journey to dreamland is full of adventures, but God has promised; "I will never leave thee, nor forsake thee" Hebrews 13:8. If you hold on a little longer, you will discover that you were not far from reaching your dream, after all.

"In every battle, there comes a time when both sides consider themselves beaten, then he who continues the attack wins." These are the words of America's 18th President–Ulysses S. Grant. Grant served as a gallant soldier during the Civil War, scoring much success; he was finally promoted to the rank of Captain in 1853. The year following his promotion Grant resigned from the army. He left the Army after being accused of drinking on duty. Then he struggled for seven years, barely able to support his family. On April 12, 1861, Grant volunteered his military service, and initially, he was rejected. With the help of an Illinois congressman, Grant was appointed the commander of the 21st Illinois volunteer regiment. In 1869 Grant was elected president at only 46 years of age–he goes in history as the fourth-youngest president in the United States.

"Then he who continues the attack wins" I'm persuaded to think that those words define the success philosophy of Grant. Life can be so harsh and challenging, but if you continue to fight, you'll win eventually. This man could have lost hope, but because of persistence, he became the President of the United States.

Do you know what you can become if you hold on? The road will not be easy, but if you continue to attack, you will win.

What To Do When The Road Seems So Tough

There are several strategies or practices you can employ that will tremendously help you cope with severe events in your life:

1.   **The practice of realizing a greater understanding of yourself and the world around you**: You must understand that events in your life don't define who you are. Yes, you might have made mistakes, but that is not who you are. You must have a correct understanding of your true identity. You should be at peace with yourself and the world around you. You have no control over things that come your way so don't bother yourself too much. Instead focus on those things that are within your power to manage, control and change.

2.   **The practice of looking within until you find the source of your suffering**: When we allow fear to govern our lives, we become wrecks. Eleanor Roosevelt said that "You gain strength, courage, and confidence by every

experience in which you really stop to look in the face. You are able to say to yourself; I lived through this horror, I can take the next thing that comes along". You must overcome your inner fears and learn to face your fears. Fear often paralyzes your efforts to a better self. Usually, what you may be afraid of is afraid of you. Release your fears and start living.

3.   **The practice of realizing that you are perfectly whole**: God has fully equipped you with all you require for a successful life. The problem is that you doubt and think less of yourself. You have all it takes. Let me say this that if you lack anything, it's because you have not used what you already have. Say you are ignorant about something; God already gave you a mind to read, investigate, and research. You are perfectly whole and not in any need of what it takes to realize your dreams. I dare you to believe – you are perfectly whole.

4.   **The practice of intentional solitude**: some refer to it as meditation; a reflection or quiet time etc. solitude is an essential practice for anyone who desires to make any meaningful impact. Solitude gives you the chance to internalize and conduct some personal inventory by asking soul-searching questions. From time to time, you must take some days off from all manner of distractions and focus on

nothing else but self.

Helen Keller once said that "Although the world is full of suffering, it is also full of the overcoming of it." How beautiful are those words? You can choose what to do with what life throws at you. The point is that you must never see your challenges as disadvantages. Instead, you need to realize that your experience facing and overcoming adversity is one of your most significant advantages.

So, don't waste time to pray for a life free of challenges because God will not answer such a prayer. If at all He answers such a prayer, He will say, "My grace is sufficient." You have the strength to overcome; take courage, and fight.

Problems don't come to kill you; instead, they come to build and prepare you for your destiny. Friends don't be afraid of the divine route; it is your highway to reaching your future safe and sound. Never give in to the temptation of settling for the normal status quo. Joseph pilgrimed that divine route though not understanding the turns and twists, he trusted and remained faithful to God and his dream.

Around 2 am walking from a bus station called Big Bite in Kabwe, Zambia, coming from getting my sister I assured her that unlike Lusaka Kabwe night streets were safe. She was coming from crisscrossing the nation seeking entry into Nursing School. The national tour ended in disappointment, but today I know God had a better path for her. The dream of nursing was becoming dim by each passing day.

When I visited their home in Livingstone some years after, we sat talking computer codes; the nurse was then studying IMIS (Institute for Management of Information System). Fast forward on the details; today, she is running Sho'dol cosmetics. What about nursing? Nursing is a profession within the health care sector focused on the care of individuals, families, and communities so they may attain, maintain, or recover optimal health and quality of life.

We can say nursing is care. Think of it, helping ladies to feel good and confident about themselves is undoubtedly improving the quality of their lives.

As of 2016, she was doing a Diploma in Skin Care and said to me that she was planning to come back to Zambia to build a skincare hospital. So if you ask me what her purpose is, Emma's purpose is to build people's self-esteem and confidence through skin-care.

For you, my reader, life may seem to force you out of your ambitioned path, well, sometimes the way to your dreams is that way. Remember, Joseph's dreamed that he was exalted above his brothers and parents, but life took him to a place that was so different. In Egypt, he couldn't see how his dream would come true. The brothers to kneel before him were thousands of miles away. But God in His wisdom knows the END from the BEGINNING – TRUST HIM.

That is how the divine route appears. Decide to go with God no matter which place life takes you.No matter the mountains to climb, valleys to endure and rivers to cross, you will go Above and Beyond to reach your dreams.

CHAPTER FOUR

MIND YOUR BUSINESS

"Failure to mind your business is your weakness you are failing to manage." – Andrew Mudolo

One of the greatest mistakes of most readers of Bible characters is the immortalization of the people they read about. By crowning the biblical figure with sainthood usually overshadows the lessons to be learned from their errors and mistakes. If the Bible records the weaknesses of these all-time people, why then should we overlook those gray areas? Joseph has a defect that most readers never pay attention to.

"And Joseph brought unto his father their evil report". Genesis 37:2. Here we see revealed one of Joseph's weaknesses; he went about badmouthing his brothers to the father.

Firstly, this backbiting was done to maintain the favor

Joseph enjoyed with his father, trying by all means to remain Dad's favorite son.

Secondly, it exhibits the lack of wisdom on Joseph part at the time.

Joseph was still in the competition of teenage sibling and rivalry. Lynne Griffin says, "Nothing causes more short and long-term damage to the sibling dynamic than comparing academic or extracurricular achievements."

It is often a parent's approval or disapproval that sparks sibling rivalry.

The fact is that kids will get into it with each other from time to time. There is a whole of things the can breed sibling rivalry: toys, school lunches, bed preferences, home chaos, etc. There's probably no way to eliminate siblings arguing with each other entirely. If parents are observant and deliberate about managing sibling rivalry, it can be very productive for the children. Each child needs to learn to stand up for himself and to take care of himself, so you can let them battle it out to a point. But you should never let it escalate to levels of name-calling, fighting, or bad-mouthing.

What we should realize is that Joseph was not this ten-year-old boy being manhandled by his elder brothers; he was seventeen years of age.

The shepherd business accorded the brothers some moments of leisure, and I believe this leisure time his brothers appreciated is what displeased Joseph to such an extent that he reported to his father. This badmouthing made a spy of Joseph, always looking for the wrongs of his brothers and overlooked anything good they did. And of course, what the father got was a report of his sons not being serious about the family business. It only fueled the hatred and cruelty of his brothers.

Friends, you must avoid at all cost the unnecessary fighting for recognition within the family; it only leads to striving and hatred.

Such an environment of strive and hatred can set in motion a vicious cycle of tragic events as you will see later in the life of Joseph. Remember, the first murder ever in the history of humanity was fueled by such competition and jealous. Cain was jealous of his brother; the jealous was so intense that it gave birth to a gruesome murder. Genesis 4:3–8.

Amid the hostility that now saturated the relationship between Joseph and his brothers, he then goes on to share his dreams with them. What an unwise move. What was he expecting from his brothers? Jubilation? I believe this shows another of Joseph's failures and weakness; the young man had an undiscerning heart. Knowing who to share your dreams with matters, but Joseph took his dreams as if everyone would celebrate it. Even at the birth of our Lord Jesus, God only chose to share this wonderful news with the shepherds while Herod remained in darkness concerning the matter.

Undiscerning, the wise men misapplied their wisdom by going to the Palace to look for the child Jesus and thereby alerting Herod the great who felt that his reign was threatened.

Herod planned to kill the baby Jesus, which was exactly what Joseph's brothers did in selling him; killing him and forever doing away with the possibility of his dreams coming to pass. Who are you sharing your dreams and life's aspirations with?

Find for yourself a mentor and life coach to whom you can be committed to and who will, in turn, be committed to you.

This is the person to give you council concerning your dreams and aspirations. Value their opinion so much so that you will not take any significant step in your journey without seeking their counsel.

Be wise and avoid competition and strive in business, family, or church but always understand that other people are there for your learning and improvement and not as rivals. Minding your own business is vital to stay focused and determined on your personal goals. On your journey to your dreamland always strive to minimize and eliminate your weaknesses and substantially invest in cultivating and growing your strengths.

Helpful Tips For Managing Sibling Rivalry

This section is essential for parents who seek to learn how to help their children differ without hurting each other. Here are five keys to help you achieve your goal of managing sibling rivalry: Talk, Teach, Reinforce, Exemplify, and Acknowledge.

1.   **Talk**: Most parents, unfortunately, don't know the difference between yelling and talking. In most cases, parents fall into the trap of just yelling instead of talking. In a normal tone, tell your child the wrong, giving reasons why it is wrong. After that, suggest the right thing and leave them to think about what you've said. The talk should flow back and forth – questions, suggestions, answer, etc. I present this to you as the first step.

2.   **Teach**: By teaching, I mean, don't only talk to your children when there is a wrong done. Don't be reactive rather be proactive — deliberately set time to teach your children values, norms, discipline, and beliefs. Doing so

instills positive action that overcomes competition. This too, should have the child's full participation – give them a chance to contribute.

3.   **Reinforce**: To ensure that the values, norms, disciplines, and beliefs that you are teaching find expression in action set forth reinforcement programs. One of these programs could be having the kids celebrate together the achievement of one of them. Let every child be involved in their sibling's activities. If one of the kids plays soccer; to reinforce your teaching, take the whole family to go and cheer for their brother or sister.

4.   **Exemplify**: If your children think you are a saint and they are the little devils, then you will never achieve your goal. You must let the children know your own mistakes and those of people they know, e.g., uncles, cousins, etc. That will help them gain a sense of hope – if they feel that they are cursed little troublemakers, then they will follow that order.

5.   **Acknowledge**: Usually, your kids feel certain emotions which lead to and when they engage in sibling rivalry. You have to acknowledge your child's feelings and further continue to encourage them to share with you. If kids are hiding their emotions, then you will not effectively solve or manage their relationships with each other. Let

them know it is alright to feel anger, disgust, disappointment, pain, etc. and you can do that by acknowledging their feelings and allowing them to talk about it.

Stop Being A Busybody

From what I have observed, many people usually take offense when you ask them to mind their own business. They fill that their 'busybody' activities are a manifestation of their concern.

Many people would not agree that they are busybodies. If you are not a busy body, then you are a person who minds his/her own business. The term busybody usually implies a person who is intent on the private matters of other people but looks a little at his issues.

There is a tendency by busybodies to focus on the faults, foibles, and troubles of other people.

Do you find yourself bothered about knowing the intimate details of your workmate, a neighbor's etc.? The graphic picture of being a busybody is what Jesus gave; "You hypocrite, first take the plank out of your eye, and then you will see clearly to move the speck from your brother's eye" (see Matthew 7:5, NIV).

A busybody is a person with a sinful curiosity. They make

inquiries into other people's private life with a sense of intrusion.

We live in a world of problems and troubles all around – marriages breaking, wife abuse, children lack respect for parents and failures of all kind. For many people, these challenges are instead kept private. With insincere concern a busybody asks, wanting more details and the next minute they are all over badmouthing and spreading all manner of gossip.

The privilege you gain from seeing other people's troubles and problems are so that you can be a channel of encouragement and not discouragement.

The faults and sins you observe in other people should make you reflect on your own life. Before you rush into condemning your fellow, check your own life because you might be worse than them. Let other people's weaknesses, failures, mistakes be a learning point for you. Remember, I want to help you go above and beyond. To make sense of your destiny journey, you've got to go above your prejudice and learn to be gracious to other people.

Failure to mind your own business and being a busybody can affect your life negatively. Let me highlighted some ways how this happens:

1.   **Lack of Focus on personal development**: One of

the indispensable qualities and disciplines required for you to achieve your dream and purpose is that of unwavering focus. Maintaining your focus is essential to a productive life. There are many distractions in this life. It is easy for you to manage distractions coming from other people, but the ones coming from within may not be easy. Instead of focusing on how you can develop your life, you become overshadowed by watching other people. Don't behave like a police officer; inspecting people to the later. It is not your job to do so. Your job is to examine your own life and ensuring that it remains on course. Jack Canfield said, "Successful people maintain a positive focus in life no matter what is going around them. They stay focused on their past success rather than their past failures, and on the next action steps they need to take to get them closer to the fulfillment of their goals rather than all the other distractions that life presents to them". For sure life presents a lot of distractions, and one of those distractions is being a busybody.

2.   **Creation of unnecessary enemies**: Like we have seen in the story of Joseph; he made enemies of his brother because he failed to mind his own business. It is surprising how people go about badmouthing their colleagues to their bosses and then wonder when they are given the cold

shoulder by everyone else. You can spare yourself a lot of heartache and drama by avoiding the trap of being a busybody.

Do you know that wisdom is highly-priced and rare to find? Most people make a wreck of their lives because of the lack of it. When it comes to minding your own business; wisdom demands that you exercise restraint.

When you decide to poke your nose in other people's businesses, don't cry when you get a bleeding nose.

Don't waste your time being a busybody; learn to focus on matters that are relevant to your dream and the journey that leads to it. Like I said early, I want you to do yourself a favor and learn to focus on the plunk in your eye and not the speck in your brother's eye.

Anytime you get the temptation of investigating into other people's lives, remember that you may be carrying a plunk in your own life. If you deal with the plunk in your own life; it is almost automatic that people with specks find themselves sharing their struggles and secrets to you for advice. So, get busy minding your own business and stop being a busybody.

No matter your weakness and shortcomings, you will go Above and Beyond to reach your dreams.

"Most of the trouble in this world has been caused by folks

who can't mind their own business, because they have no business of their own to mind, any more than a smallpox virus has" – William S. Burroughs

CHAPTER FIVE

WHAT WILL YOUR DREAM PROVOKE?

"Your dream will provoke favor or fight; it will attract sponsors or slanderers, celebrations, or criticisms. You will either provoke anyone or both sides." – Andrew Mudolo

Joseph dreamt, and he shared his dreams, then the trouble started. Critics and haters that surround you get even more menace when they hear your dreams, goals, and plans. If you aim high expect difficulty from those, who see you on a lower level. Joseph in the eyes of his brothers was this spoiled, lazy young brother and the thought of him reigning over them was more egregious than the initial position they had towards him. It is always crucial in destiny's journey to remember that not everyone will celebrate you. If you are expecting everybody, you see to like you, you in for a shock.

The sooner you get this into the emotional system, the easier it will be for you to overcome discouragements on destiny's journey.

"And his brethren envied him, but his father observed the saying." Genesis 37:11

Dreams produce envy in those who see you as going nowhere. What exactly is it that his brothers felt. The feeling was that of longing to possess the advantage Joseph had. The Meaning of the dreams was not hidden from them. They knew what the dreams meant, and they longed to be in Joseph shoes. They probably interpreted his dreams as Joseph inheriting the entire wealth of their father. I would imagine them thinking, "why does it have to be him and not me? The more they thought of Joseph's dreams, the more the hatred swelled up in their hearts. At this moment, the desire to kill was conceived, and anyone who hates a brother or sister is a murderer, and you know very well that eternal life and murder don't go together. Anyone who keeps hatred is capable of killing given a chance. The Dreamer is the object of hatred and to the hater; all they desire is to get rid of the object. The ten brothers envisioned Joseph's future success and accomplishments, and they didn't take it too well. So the next time you embark on a money-making idea, or wedding, career change, ministry, etc. remember that trouble will start. Joseph's enemies were those of his household. Caution must be borne in mind regarding those with whom you share your plans, aspirations, and hope in life. Not everyone is happy for you, and it is worse when they are in the inner circle of your life.

Furthermore, Joseph's brothers developed a restless desire to acquire their brother's status, and if not, it would make them happy to see him lose it.

"If I can't have it, then no one should," that's the feeling that Joseph's siblings developed towards him."

The most common thing among men is that they are always ready to give up their dreams and ambitions to pursue another person's. A man discontent with his lot in life will endeavor to step into another's dream with a view of satisfying his craving for accomplishment and recognition. The breed of discontent individuals is mainly responsible for stepping into other people's businesses instead of minding their own.

In reading Joseph's story, never miss the importance of what is said concerning his father's position when he learned of his favorite son's dreams; Jacob pondered deeply on these dreams even though he appeared to everyone as having ostracized Joseph.

His mind brooded over those dreams like a hen over her eggs; protecting and providing the right temperature for hatching. When Jacob cried over the news of his favorite son Joseph's death, am convinced his tears were for a lost future his son had. He thought of the Sun, Moon and eleven stars bowing to Joseph's star, oh what pain of loss. How the mighty have fallen was the father's cry. There will be people who will always hold dear to their hearts the dreams you share with them as if the dreams were their own.

They will meditate on them and give you positive feedback required to improve your chances of success in your dreamland.

What You Need To Know About Criticism

What is the source of criticism? Can you live a life free of criticism? If you are a person who feels that you need to live in such a way that will never attract criticism, then you are mistaken.

The truth is that no matter how you choose to live your life – whether you build a business or work a regular job; marry or stay single, lose or gain weight; be good or bad – whatever you do, someone will judge you for it. The problem is not what you do but what others think of what you do. People will always find a reason to project their insecurities, their negativity, and their fears onto you and your life. What you need is to know how to deal with it. When you envision something big in life, people will criticize you. They will judge your ability, education, commitment to making the dream become a reality. Due to the scope of the book, I'll not focus on self-criticism.

Negative criticism is a deadly poison that can endanger your dreams. But let me remind you in the words of Aristotle; "There is only one way to avoid criticism: do nothing, say nothing and be nothing." In simple terms, even if you die, people will criticize you. So to avoid it, don't exist. The fact that you are reading this book is enough evidence that you have either encountered or yet to confront criticism. If you go about it the wrong way; you will hold back your required effort for dream realization.

How do you handle Criticism?

This is the big question. I have shown you that as long as you are alive, everything you do will attract criticism – Negative, Positive, or even both forms of criticisms.

1.   Criticism is someone's opinion of who you are and what you do. It may be true or false; therefore don't let it define you. If it is true; it allows you to improve. If it is false, trash it. Let it not DEFINE you!

2.   Allow criticism to give you a different perspective

on your dreams and your life in general. Instead of being crushed by negative criticism, use it as a platform for conducting an inventory of your own life. GET A PERSPECTIVE.

3.   Don't be too hard on yourself. In the face of negative criticism, people frequently fall into the trap of condemning themselves. TAKE IT EASY.

4.   Criticism is like a dumbbell, if you don't handle it well, it can hurt you, but if you take control of it and learn how to work with it, it will build a bicep. TAKE CONTROL.

You either let the criticism control you – or you can take control of the criticism. The choice is yours.

I want to highlight to you my reader at this juncture a critical point. Joseph's brothers were envious of his dreams, but his father, on the other hand, had an internal appreciation of the whole matter.

I would like for you to appreciate these two factors in our journey to destiny. The Critics and the Celebrators; every destiny has a critic and thank God every destiny has a Celebrator. Through these avenues, God accomplishes his purpose in his children. Joseph undiscerning mind led him to share with his brothers (critics) what he should have only shared with his father (celebrator).

I want to make this observation here that, even if Joseph was not sold by his brother's, he would have still ended up the governor of Egypt.

Suffice to say that some hard lessons of life you have encountered were a result of your own making but thank God that He still takes our mistakes and turns them for our good. Bruce Lee was right when he said; "Mistakes are always forgivable if one dares to admit them." Usually, people have a hard time forgiving themselves. My dear, don't let self-blame eat you up; release yourself from the pain of mistakes you've made in the past. You need to know that past your mistakes; you can start all over again!

Turn your mess into a message. "And we know that all things work together for good to them that love God, to them who are the called according to his purpose." Romans 8:28. Paul here says "and we know..." Do you know? Do you know that the happenings of your life will work out for good because you love God?

Joseph reached this knowledge in his life, he said to his brothers; "And Joseph said unto them, Fear not: for am I in place of God? Genesis 50:19–21.

Without the climax of such knowledge, you will go about carrying bitterness and revenge, and sadly that may become your new dream –bitterness, and revenge. God is the only judge.

The day you decide to share your dream, you will stir up all manner of responses from people around you. Some will respond positively by encouraging, advising, financing, or promoting it. On the other hand, your dream will stimulate negative responses which manifest in slander, negative criticism, etc. it is vital to expect negative criticism and prepare for it. When it comes to positive responses, make room for them too, and never let them cause you to lose your focus; don't grow big-headed when people celebrate your dreams.

Provocation Is The Nature Of Dreams

If you want to start a fight, have a dream, and be determined to pursue it regardless the odds. If you want people to call you all manner of names, dare to dream. The day you start dreaming you will attract all manner of reactions; both positive and negative. On the other hand, if you dream and determine to pursue it regardless of the odds, you will attract favor.

If you have a dream, people want to see how prepared you are to stick to it. Commitment to a cause will provoke people's hearts to favor your cause. This is one principle politicians apply in the quest to win an election. A politician that shows the determination for a purpose he stands for will eventually win the hearts and favor of the people.

This is how Africans got their independence. They did it through the commitment of a few people who dreamed of freedom. To win people's favor and have them buy into your dream, prove to them that you are 100% committed to your dream. The flip side to that is that when people perceive your commitment to your dream; they step up advances that would pull you down. People who are envious of your dreams will undoubtedly bully you. You must expect verbal bullying from people who fight your dreams. Verbal bullying includes withholding information, name-calling and hurtful labeling, and many others all with the intended purpose of degrading you. Those fighting your dreams do these things in the hope that you will relent from believing and following after your dreams.

Verbal bullies will say things like:

• Who do you think you are?

• Others have tried what makes you think you can do it?

• You are not qualified.

• What have you ever accomplished, Mr. Failure?

• Be realistic?

• It can never be done.

- You are wasting your time.

- It is far beyond your reach.

- You are too young/ old to attempt such a thing.

To go above and beyond barricades erected by those who have decided to give you the bitter pill on account of your dream, you need to fortify yourself mentally and emotionally.

Let me share some helpful tips on how you can fence out all such projections:

1. **Believe in yourself**: The Bible will give witness to the fact that God's biggest problems are not the challenges men face but men themselves. God appeared to Moses, Gideon, Joshua, and many other Bible characters, and the first response they give to an assignment of national transformation is; "Go and find some else." They offer every excuse in the book. The truth is that failure to believe in yourself will lead to unfulfilled dreams. So, friends dare to believe in yourself. For your information, God believes in you; that's why he has entrusted you with that great dream. No one can make you inferior unless you allow them to. Dare to believe in yourself!

2. **Believe in your potential**: You need to believe that you are divinely equipped for your dream. Whatever you require making your dream come true is all within you.

Discover, Develop, and sharpen every endowment you possess. Many people will try to convince you that you don't have what it takes to realize your dream. Friend, never allow any such insinuations. Dare to believe in your potential.

3.   **Don't reason a belittling opinion**: Don't reason with belittling opinions of people; never give a chance to such comments in the name of humility.

It's not being humble sitting and listening to people poisoning you. You must be intelligent enough to tell the difference between positive criticism and poisoning negative comments. Sometimes the negative comments will appear like genuine concern. Beware!

I want to conclude this chapter with an emphasis on positive and negative criticism. I'll base it on a review of Winston Churchill's words. Winston Churchill once said, "Criticism may not be agreeable, but it is necessary. It fulfills the same function as pain in the human body. It calls attention to an unhealthy state of things". It is cardinal to realize that both positive and negative criticism come to challenge your ideas, character or ability. The second thing both share in common is that they both can hurt. Positive criticism even when it hurts stems from a sincerer heart of concern and help, it boosts your self-esteem. On the other hand, negative criticism stems from the ill motive, and its goal is to crush your enthusiasm; it lowers your self-esteem.

When you dream, the two forms of criticisms will appear, and it is up to you to know what to entertain and what to dismiss. Expect the negative but feed on the positive, that's my creed for life.

No Matter your mistakes, people's hatred
and criticism you will go Above and
Beyond to reach your dreams.

CHAPTER SIX

HANDLING INJECTIONS OF REJECTION

"A stab in the back is usually from those that don't matter, but a stub in the chest right to the heart usually is from those we love; close friends and family" – Andrew Mudolo

Channing Pollock once said, "The only good luck many great men ever had was being born with the ability and determination to overcome bad luck." Joseph had his share of bad luck. Joseph thought it was another one of his dreams; his brothers pouncing on him like a pack of hungry wolves. His teenage mind could not absorb the shock of this horrific act of injustice towards him. "Maybe they are just toying with me," he comforted himself in the shadows of the dry well.

In a little while, hope revived, and an assuring thought of

his brothers' love grew as they pulled him out of that pit. Well, it was an experience short-lived as he heard them transacting with the Ishmaelite traders. The brothers that should have shown great love and care for their young brother had just reduced him to a mere commodity.

In life beloved reader many people will treat you like that; employers will see you as a mere tool, the government will count you are as a mere statistic and even your family may consider you just a commodity. I have often seen and heard of such stories were parents sell young girls off into marriage; it is sad.

People can go to unthinkable lengths to acquire money, but for Joseph's brothers, it was more than the money they wanted. All they wanted was to lose sight and thought of this "pain" in their lives. "If we are to get rid of this boy, better we make a little gain on the side, draw him from the well and merchandise him to these God sent slave traders," the brothers encouraged themselves. With each mile the Ishmaelite caravans covered, the more Joseph got into despair, the dust blinding his eyes from familiar sights, oh what an agonizing ordeal. The imagination of slavery life begun to flash past his eyes, "Could this be happening to me"? "Here I am," on an unplanned journey without bidding my beloved father goodbye to an uncertain, unexpected future. Don't you fill like that sometimes? Living life with the despair of uncertainty, we can learn from what Shraga Silverstein said: "In worrying about what the future will bring we lose what the present is bringing." Don't allow yourself to drown into despondency. Free your mind of all worry, and as Joseph's story shows us; things do get better.

Rejection Is An Event

The fact is that since a young age, we have all experienced and frequently been tormented by denial. We have seen rejection crop up at school, at work, in relationships, and the pursuit of our dreams. Over the years, we have been rejected by significant others, rejected by parents, from teams, from programs, from projects, from companies, from roles, from organizations, and institutions. Rejection is a reality of life hence the need to educate ourselves about it as we strive to go 'above and beyond.'

One thing is sure; in life, you will experience one form of rejection or another. What is essential to know and realize is that rejection is an EVENT. That event could be people denying you something you require or need, e.g., a job, sexual intimacy for those in marriage or family relation as seen in the case of Joseph. What we famous call 'feeling of rejection' is our responses to an event of rejection. "It's not what happens to you, but how you respond that matters" – Epictetus. That is the cardinal point to realize. It's not the divorce, the abandonment by parents, the denial of a business contract, the regret letter to your job application, instead, it is HOW you react to those events of rejection that matters. You must learn to FOCUS on your response as opposed to the actions of rejection coming from other people. You have CONTROL over your responses, but you don't have even an ounce over other people's actions.

It Hurts To Be Rejected

There is no disputing; in life, you will have trials, disappointments, and letdowns. Rejection can spur emotions that kill self-esteem and can limit your destiny. Like Joseph, your parents or siblings could have rejected you, and you have grown up feeling like the black sheep of the family. It may be rejection in marriage by a beloved spouse, a person you have devoted your whole life to till death. The easy way out could be to commit suicide, which is an option for the weak, fainthearted, and irresponsible.

But you can also decide to respond positively to the negative circumstances you encounter in your life. Imagine you are rushing to respond to a knock at the door of your house when suddenly you hit your little toe into the edge of the wall. There is such a pain that almost causes your heart to jump out of your body. Say you are trying to put a nail on the wall on which you could hang a portrait. Imagine you miss the head of the nail and find your finger instead. Social rejection produces the same effect as those events. When you experience a breakup in a romantic relationship, it hurts, when you are treated as the black sheep of the family; that too hurts.

Yes, when you are fired from your job, it hurts. It hurts, because of experiences of social rejection, when elicited powerfully enough, recruit brain regions involved in both the affective and sensory components of physical pain. Thus social rejection is as damaging as physical injury.

Ethan Kross; professor of Psychology at the University of Michigan Emotion and Self-Control Laboratory together with a team of fellow scientists, discovered that the same areas of our brain become activated when we experience rejection as when we experience physical pain.

That's why even small rejections hurt more than we think they should because they elicit literal (albeit, emotional) pain. Just like we protect ourselves and our loved ones from physical harm, we all should strive to protect them from social rejection as well. Physical pain may be apparent, but it's an emotional pain of social rejection that we must carefully watch for because it mostly goes unnoticed.

Core Beliefs About Rejection

Rational Emotive Behavioral Therapy (REBT) is a tool founded Albert Ellis in which he posits that the reason that people felt what they felt after a rejection event has to do with their underlying beliefs & philosophies about getting the approval, companionship, support, intimacy, etc. of another.

Rejection can be experienced when you are not accepted into a relationship, or when you are discarded or when you are put out or perhaps considered as useless. This kind of treatment has pushed people to become wrecks in life who end up transferring their pain onto innocent others. The reason for the pain and hurt is underlying beliefs and philosophies. Of course, we are created as social beings with a need for love and attachment.

Humanity craves a sense of belonging, which if denied, violates our emotions. In relationships where there is this sense of belonging, humans express their love, joys, success, and all the accomplishments.

Furthermore, these relationships accord the chance for people to express fears, failures, and plans for the future. So when a person is cut from this essential need, there is disorientation amid all manner of insecurities in an individual. This too can hinder a person from realizing dreams and aspirations.

Cognitive therapists Aaron and Judith Beck identified three categories of core beliefs that I would like to share with you.

1.   **Unloveability**: Take, for example, in 'Relational Rejection' say in divorce. You may tend to believe that the reason for the rejection is that you are unlovable or undesirable. Many people move about feeling unloved because their spouse divorced them. The result is they fail to invest full commitment into any other relationship because of this feeling. The event took place as a one-off time, but it permanently impacted their belief system. Thus for such a person to overcome rejection, they need to know and believe that they are lovable and that that one experience of divorce is not what should define their life. You might have gone through a bitter divorce but your name and identity is not 'divorcee.'

2.   **Inadequacy**: Let's cite an example of 'Occupational Rejection' say in dismissal. When a person experiences a job loss, it is usually that they begin to see themselves as victims of other people's perception of their inadequacy. Experiencing Occupational Rejection may prevent an individual from making attempts at other job

opportunities because he/she now believes that he/she is less capable. I earlier spoke about Oprah – Oprah Winfrey was hired as the co-anchor of 6 pm newscast in 1977. She had just come to Baltimore when she was 22 years old. Oprah recounts that just seven and a half months later, after a big promotional buildup, Oprah experience what can be termed as the first and worst failure of her TV career. Instead of wallowing in a pool of rejection grief Oprah went above and beyond occupational rejection, and she attests to this when she says "By the time I left Baltimore, I was solidly aware that I no longer wanted to do television news. I was very uncomfortable doing television news". What should have crushed her spirit became the energy she needed to push to the next level.

3.   **Unworthiness**: I would like us to consider the example of 'Action Rejection'. This is rejection resulting from a lousy action you did which may, in turn, make you feel unworthy, immoral, or corrupt. Many people after serving a prison sentence, feel almost condemned for life. In some countries, ex-convicts can get a job; they are released to find their spouse married and moved on. People readily welcome them into their homes, fearing the unknown. Thus wrong actions we do can spur emotions of rejection and cause problems in the future.

How to overcome rejection

Only the presence of Hope overcomes rejection. "… and there is a friend that sticketh closer than a brother". Proverbs 18:24. "Let your conversation be without covetousness; and be content with such things as ye have: for he hath said, I will never leave thee, nor forsake thee." No matter the rejection, God has promised to always be with you. Christ is our ever-present help and friend in all situations. He is an all-weather friend, never to leave nor forsake you. You can count on Him when all else fails. Now I know this may not sound practical to you, so I want to present to you reasonable steps and ways which can help you to overcome rejection.

1.   **Realize that things can go wrong**: my friends we are not in a perfect world; therefore, you must learn to anticipate not only the good things of life. In life, you will experience troubles. Be prepared. Most people are negatively affected by rejection because it pounces on the like a thief in the night. They don't expect it. Yes, you don't always have to be a person who preaches doomsday but realizes that the fact that the term exists suggests that one day might and will be doomsday. Be prepared even for the worst of developments.

2.   **Realize that it is not the end of the world**: When

you hit rock bottom when you experience rejection, know that it is not the end of the world. There is still a life to pursue after that episode of rejection. Today we cry, but tomorrow is another day – let's give life another shot.

3.   **Realize that you still have worth**: Your self-image and confidence can be affected mainly by rejection. Therefore, you need to know how to maintain your self-esteem, self-confidence, and positive self-image. Rejection does not mean you are worthless it just means that the person or entity rejecting you do not know how valuable you are – and you can't blame them for that, and neither should you blame yourself.

4.   **Realize your lessons**: Life is a school, and one of the standard exams in this school is called rejection. There are lessons to be learned from an event of rejection; could it be that you didn't put your best effort? Perhaps you overlooked something. Whatever the case, learn from the event and do better.

There is no easy way to handle rejection but there is undoubtedly a way. Remember rejection hurts and the pain of rejection only stops when you stop being a victim and start taking charge of your life. Rejection should not relegate you to a pity party; instead, it should lead you into a glorious triumph. The key is that you must decide to stop being the opinion of other people and start living your life. Go Above and Beyond bitter rejection to attain your dreams

"We all learn lessons in life. Some stick, some don't. I have always learned more from rejection and failure than from acceptance and success" – Henry Rollins

CHAPTER SEVEN

PROSPERING IN EVERY SEASON OF YOUR DREAM

"What you do prospers, and what you don't do does not prosper" – Andrew Mudolo

Everyone wants to prosper. Parents are continually pushing their children to go to school, work hard, and get a promising career. When the children grow up to think for themselves they develop dreams of their own; dreams of cars, houses, women, jewelry, and all manner of icons of material wealth. There is a whole industry dedicated to developing and teaching prosperity. In the religious circles, we have seen the rise of the prosperity gospel, which is nothing but a cheap scam to defraud God's people of their hard-earned money. People are always looking and anxiously waiting for the season that will enable them to prosper. Yes, there is a season and a time for everything, but you can choose to prosper at whatever level you find yourself.

By implication, prosperity entails – being successful, continuously flourishing, and general well-being. Everyone is pursuing that prosperity even though some may be seeking it unconsciously.

Prosperity entails physical, economic, and social wellness. Prosperity also involves the achievement of a predetermined activity. Joseph's success was not a function of magic or chance; reading his story, you observe that it was not accidental. It seems as though Joseph had a formula for prosperity. Joseph's success was a function of principles. Principles are absolute; if you try to change or frustrate them, they can damage your life, but when you cooperate with laws, they make your endeavors excel. What was Joseph's secret? In Potiphar's house, he prospered, in prison, he excelled above his fellows, and when he became governor, he governed with the same result – Excellence.

In the face of a closed door, possessing the right key is the first concern to occupy the mind of anyone who desires passage through that door. Many people in life are waiting for the appearance of an open door, not realizing that in their hands, God has placed the right key that opens the closed door that is before them.

When God created you, he put in you the resources required to change the situations that arise on your journey while relying on Him for wisdom on decisions that you are taking to transform those situations.

Joseph mastered the key and used it effectively, and he succeeded at whatever level in his life. Why are you just sitting there and crying, Joseph had every reason to complain, but he acted differently.

He chose to adapt to the environment, mastered it and flourished under the circumstance that many would have accepted as being the status quo. He used the key in his hands to rise to the top even when the top meant the lowest of positions he had imagined.

He fought language barriers, climbed mountains of sectarian violence, and intimidation to become Potiphar's trusted servant overseeing his entire master's estate.

In this generation of pleasure and leisure, very few people are putting their best in their chosen field of endeavor. Preachers, accountants, lawyers, teachers, and many others are putting in less than the average of what their training, salary, the potential is worth. Non–Christians and Christians alike are living below their potential, but for a believer, it is a sin to live below the deposits of God in you. Hard work should not be confused with the curse of laborious sweat. It is not a curse overshadowing people outside of God's grace revealed in Jesus Christ. Hard work is only doing the best possible; this entails a full deployment of your talents, energies, skills, time, and all potentials. I like saying it this way;

> ***"If anyone can do it, I can do good, if nobody can do it, I can do it better, and if I can't-do it, then I can do best."***

Joseph's success key was work, he did something, and God

prospered what he did. If you are sitting, then you are giving God nothing to prosper.

Consider Deuteronomy 2:7 "For the LORD thy God hath blessed thee in all the works of thy hand: he knoweth thy walking through this great wilderness: these forty years the LORD thy God hath been with thee; thou hast lacked nothing." "Bless thee in all the works of thy hand"

The works of your hands are the means through which God's blessing is actuated in your life.

Are you in lack? According to God's word, the reason is that you are not doing any work. The children of Israel worked, God-blessed, and the result was that they lacked nothing. The more work you do, the more platform you create for the expression of the blessing of God in your life.

As a child of God, you are a blessed child, but what makes the difference between the needy and the abounding child of God is work. God works, and Jesus works, why do you expect anything less? "But Jesus answered them, My Father worketh hitherto, and I work." John 5: 17.

The enemy wants you to work for nothing, but as sure as the morning rise, your hard work shall pay off. Joseph worked hard in Potiphar's house and excelled above his fellows. Even in prison, his hard work materialized in his promotion to a prison official, in–charge of his fellows. Work and keep working and so shall your increase materialize and you will not lack. Make a firm resolve to be a workaholic.

"Your work is going to fill a large part of your life, and the only way to be truly satisfied is to do what you believe is great work. And the only way to do great work is to love what you do. If you haven't found it yet, keep looking. Don't settle. As with all matters of the heart, you'll know when you find it" – Steve Jobs.

I believe the words of Steve Jobs rightly express Joseph's attitude towards work. From the promotions Joseph enjoyed at every level of his life, I'm convinced he had grown to love the work he was doing. I believe he loved to work in Potiphar's house. Even though it was not his dream job, Joseph worked as though he was the owner of the house and all its properties. When in prison, he didn't slug in a corner complaining about how life was unfair; instead, he loved to work, and the prison officers began to find him useful. WORK, WORK, WORK… Some people dream of success and prosperity, while others wake up and work hard to make it happen. Have you woken up and working to make your dream happen?

Many people block their prosperity because they think that they are only prosperous when they have reached their dreams; thus, they tend to turn down smaller opportunities that could have laid them to their dreamland. Never despise humble beginnings. It is only when you've proven faithful in little things that you can be trusted with much. Don't make the mistake of turning down seemingly meager opportunities just because you have big dreams. Take the smaller opportunities and use them to get to your bigger dreams. Let me clarify for you a most misunderstood quote. Robert Kiyosaki says, "People who dream small dreams continue to live as small people." Unfortunately, people have misunderstood that quote, and it has done more harm than good to their dreams. The correct understanding is that: Dreams are what ultimately influence the outcome of your life. The life you are living is the product of your dreams and to an extent, the lack of dreams. You can live small but dream big – in this case, your dream is what will drive you from smallness into the bigness of your dreams. You can start small but don't let your dream become small. Most people I know and read about have grown into their prosperity, they didn't just dream, and then one day it happened. They worked day after day, and when their mind was not minding prosperity and success, other people came to congratulate them. Every season in your life plays an important role; work hard and prosper in each of your life's seasons.

If you want to prosper in every season of your life:
- Discover the work you were born for
- Learn to work hard
- Learn to work smart
- Learn to love your work

And as you prosper, remember that you need to connect to and discover the absolute being. Let me share with you another of Joseph's secret. To keep going on even though the challenges he was facing is a sure testimony that Joseph had an inner flow of encouragement.

The Sweetest Of Destiny Friendships

The truth is that apart from God, you have no part in destiny and your life no matter the accomplishments. Your accomplishments culminate into meaninglessness. The legendary Dr. Myles Munroe once said the graveyard is the wealthiest place on earth; implying that many people have died without ever discovering what their purpose was. Many have died without making any contribution to the betterment of our world.

One of the reasons is that people have pursued an illusion instead of the real thing. The devil has succeeded in cheating people to believe that life is all about survival. Get educated, start earning a salary, go on and marry, have children, retire and wait for death. The world system is one of the best creations of the devil to derail you from pursuing your purpose. Most people have reduced purpose to mere survival: earning and spending.

In this world of competition, most people are drunk with success and have lost sight of the purpose. If the devil can succeed in convincing you that your life revolves around mere survival, he knows he has limited your ability to live the life God intended for you. Just listen to these words purported to be Steve Jobs' last words.

"I have come to the pinnacle of success in business. In the eyes of others, my life has been the symbol of success. However, apart from work, I have little joy. Finally, my wealth is simply a fact to which I am accustomed.

At this time, lying on the hospital bed and remembering all my life, I realize that all the accolades and riches of which I was once so proud, have become insignificant with my imminent death. In the dark, when I look at green lights, of the equipment for artificial respiration and feel the buzz of their mechanical sounds, I can feel the breath of my approaching death looming over me. Only now do I understand that once you accumulate enough money for the rest of your life, you have to pursue objectives that are not related to wealth. It should be something more important; for example, stories of love, art, dreams of my childhood. NO, stop pursuing wealth, it can only make a person into a twisted being, just like me."

These are sentiments of a life lived chasing illusions. At the end of it, there is just emptiness instead of satisfaction and fulfillment. What a big contrast with what the Apostle Paul said in 2 Timothy 4:6,7. "For I am now ready to be offered, and the time of my departure is at hand. I have fought a good fight, and I have finished my course, I have kept the faith" Paul's words are filled with a sense of satisfaction and fulfillment.

Can you see the difference between these two quotes? The first quote typifies the agony of a person pursuing SUCCESS ONLY while the other of a person seeking PURPOSE. By the way, the measure of success by God's standard always concerns your purpose. Most people will never discover late alone fulfill their purpose because they are busy pursuing an illusion: merely living to survive. There is more to life than earning, spending, marrying, having children, and retiring. To make sense of your destiny journey, you NEED to know the author of Life. You MUST fall in love with Him.

Your relationship with God through his son Jesus Christ enables you to relate to this life accordingly – that is according to His purpose and plan. God's destiny is not your portion until your life is surrendered to Jesus Christ in a loving relationship. Joseph grew up in the instructions of his father and learned all about the promises of God in his family from the time of his great-grandpa Abraham. One of the most striking statements in the life of Joseph, as found in Genesis 39:2, 21, "And the Lord was with Joseph." You should strive to work towards building such a testimony of your life. Can it be said of you that Almighty God is with you? Until your life is in the hands of God, God is not committed to bringing you into the destiny He has for your life. How can you enter God's rule? Nicodemus was told that he needed to be born again, John 3:3. Your only key to experiencing God's kingdom is by the new birth. "Fear not, little flock; for it is your Father's good pleasure to give you the kingdom." Luke 12:32. The Kingdom is God's gift to his little flock. God established earth for his kids Adam and Eve being the first generation. By living in the plan and will of God, they prospered in subduing and ruling the earth. They lived in sweet fellowship with Him. This was so for some time until the enemy of God showed the woman a counterfeit and they both; the man and woman disobeyed God and ate of the forbidden fruit and consequently lost the beautiful privilege of living the plan and will of their creator. Outside the garden, life became miserable; full of pain and tears. But thanks be to God, who even before man disobeyed a rescue plan was already in place for the restoration of God's original plan.

God's plan for creating man was not yet over. Through God's rescue plan man would continue to reflect the glory of God on earth. Jesus Christ was the secret of the rescue plan, "But we speak the wisdom of God in a mystery, even the hidden wisdom, which God ordained before the world unto our glory: Which none of the princes of this world knew: for had they known it, they would not have crucified the Lord of glory".1 Corinthians 2:7,8. The enemy thought he was finishing it all when he crucified the Lord of glory and this all scenario makes me wonder the wisdom of God in all matters; Satan is a creature and will never equal the creator. The creature can never be more significant or wiser than the creator.

The revelation of the secret plan of God for His glory through His beloved children begun with Jesus and for those who are in Christ, their lives remain a mystery to the devil and his demons. There is a life of Jesus Christ, and it is beyond any other life. It is the abundant life which He, Jesus Christ purchased with His blood. That's the life that I am presenting to you, "For the life was manifested, and we have seen it, and bear witness, and shew unto you that eternal life, which was with the Father, and was manifested unto us" 1 John 1:2. "And this is life eternal, that they might know thee the only true God, and Jesus Christ, whom thou hast sent."

This goes beyond head knowledge, but knowledge of him which result in a loving relationship with God himself and His son Jesus Christ, "That ye also may have fellowship with us: and truly our fellowship is with the Father, and with his Son Jesus Christ." 1 John 1: 3.

The life Jesus is offering you is not meaningless ritualism but meaningful relationship.

Ritualism will always lose initial zeal, but 'relationship' is continuously refueled by the revelation of the person you are relating with. Going to church, giving alms, visiting the sick, doing miracles is all meaningless when they are done out of obligation. "Whether therefore ye eat, or drink, or whatsoever ye do, do all to the glory of God" 1 Corinthians 10:31. All we do becomes meaningful when we do it in love, honoring God.

"Acquaint now thyself with him, and be at peace: thereby good shall come unto thee." Job 22: 21. Get to know the Lord, personally. Group meetings in church and community can mislead you into thinking you know the Lord, be sure that you know God. Get familiar with the ways of God; don't be a stranger to the ways of God. "He made known his ways unto Moses, his acts unto the children of Israel." Moses entered into a beautiful relationship with God, and the children of Israel only ended at just seeing the work being done and not the worker. The one was seeing God while the others saw only the hand of God. Are you seeking the hand of God or God? If you find God, you find His hand. "The people that do know their God shall be strong, and do exploits. Indeed the life of Joseph is no less than an exploit.

Joseph had a relationship with His creator and cooperated with the destiny designer, and he was able to meet life's challenges in the strength of His creator. And so you too in God's hands can conquer every mountain on your way to the destiny God has for you. If you are in doubt about your relationship with God, today can be that day.

Ask the Lord to forgive your sins, to create in you a new heart that longs after Him and His will. Surrender your life to Him and ask Him to take control of your life. Your destiny journey begins with a relationship with God and is sustained by a continuation of that relationship.

"Character cannot be developed in ease and quiet. Only through experience of trial and suffering can the soul be strengthened, ambition inspired, and success achieved" – Helen Keller

CHAPTER EIGHT

HANDLING DREAM ROBBERS AND DESTROYERS

"Temptation is an open door leading into sin, you either consciously walk through it or away from it" – Andrew Mudolo

When your destiny is gold, the temptation that the enemy brings your way are fires that can devour when you succumb. These same fires are also the fires of purification once you endure and overcome. Joseph's destiny was gold, and the enemy through Potiphar's wife conceived a mission to devour and destroy this precious destiny. Thank God Joseph overcame with terrible immediate consequences following. "And it came to pass after these things, that his master's wife cast her eyes upon Joseph; and she said, lie with me. But he refused and said unto his master's wife, Behold, my master wotteth not what is with me in the house, and he hath committed all that he hath to my hand; There is none greater in this house than I; neither hath he kept back anything from me but thee, because thou art his wife: how then can I do this great wickedness and sin against God?

And it came to pass, as she spoke to Joseph day by day, that he hearkened not unto her, to lie by her, or to be with her.

And it came to pass about this time that Joseph went into the house to do his business; and there was none of the men of the house there within. And she caught him by his garment, saying, lie with me: and he left his garment in her hand, and fled, and got him out." Genesis 40:7 – 15

You must be conscious of this fact – Like Joseph, the enemy has cast his eyes on you. The Bible says, "Watch and pray that you may not fall into temptation." If you watch, you will spot the temptation coming in, but if you siesta, you will fall. How exactly do you watch? To watch means to judge your life and environment through the mirror of God's Word. You must be vigilant to ensure that you don't set away from what you know is right and true. The devil had his eye on Job, he had his eye on Samson, he had his eye on Judas, and he certainly has his eye on you, therefore, "ye walk circumspectly, not as fools, but as wise" (see Ephesians 5:15).

I'm sure you have noticed that this woman spoke to Joseph day by day. Dear reader, the temptation will persist; the enemy will bombard you day in day out. You will receive pressure from all angles. Do you know that Joseph was a young man in his sexual prime, and this enticement presented an offer of a lifetime? With the position, Potiphar held in Egypt I'm sure his wife was a spectacle, and indeed, her beauty was nurtured and maintained with the best oils and perfumes of the Land.

Temptations come in attractive packages and sizes.

The enemy will present before you the very thing that has the highest potential to lure you into his trap and not just for a day; he will continuously present this opportunity to you peradventure your resistance drops. "Resist the devil, and he will flee from you". James 4:7. Keep the resistance, and you will emerge victoriously.

Potiphar's wife was a forbidden fruit that was presented to Joseph in the garden of his destiny. "The tree was good for food, and that it was pleasant to the eyes, and a tree to be desired to make one wise, she took of the fruit thereof and did eat..." Genesis 3:6. For a young Joseph, indeed this woman was good for food. To this mistress, Joseph was a sex novice; she could give the experience of a lifetime. She was fair to behold, and for sure, Joseph would be transformed into a real man according to the standard of the world if he only succumbed. He would have taken some and ate, but Joseph chose to run away.

The Fear Of Man Is A Trap

King Solomon says, "The fear of man bringeth a snare: but whoso putteth his trust in the LORD shall be safe." Potiphar's wife threatened Joseph that she would scream and alert people nearby. If Joseph feared Potiphar, his mistress, the prison officers or any other person, he would have easily given in to the temptation.

Joseph realized that God was always with him, and as such, he could not afford to sin against his God. Perhaps Potiphar's wife entreated him, pointing to the fact that they were alone and that their illicit act would remain a secret. Joseph didn't even give it a second thought; he knew he was in grave danger – he escaped. If Joseph feared being infected with an STI (sexually transmitted disease), he would have finally given in to the temptation, but he feared God, the alpha, and omega the one who does not change but is the same yesterday, today and forever. Your only guard in the face of temptation is the fear of God without which you are on your way to compromise.

To shun evil, one must possess the fear of God, and this is

fear born out of a vibrant relationship with Daddy God. Before Joseph resisted, he walked with God. In a previous section, I have highlighted that God was with Joseph, and that is a walk to be desired by all. God is with you when you are with him, and hence we can say Joseph's relationship with God was alive and well. Joseph's fear of the Lord was the supreme treasure that held him intact amid a proposal that may have seemed like a dream come true for countless others. But Joseph remembered that in his dream there is only Father, Mother and Brothers and no Potiphar's wife, therefore, this could not be a dream come true.

Sin is a dream robber and a dream killer; Joseph realized this critical truth; you too must come to the appreciation of this truth to secure your dream and destiny.

Moments of Pleasure

The opportunity presented to Joseph was a dream killer. Don't prostitute your dream and God-given destiny for moments of pleasure; Moses chose to suffer affliction with the people of God than to enjoy the pleasures of sin for a season. By faith Moses, when he came to years, refused to be called the son of Pharaoh's daughter; Choosing instead suffer affliction with the people of God, than to enjoy the pleasures of sin for a season. (See; Hebrews 11:24 – 25).

Dear reader, sin has pleasures, but they last only for a while.

Are you willing to suffer today to protect your future?

Are you willing to forgo today's single meal to secure a lifetime supply?

Are you willing to hold on to your birthright even if it means you starve for a while?

Are you willing to deny yourself pleasure until its due?

To overcome temptation, you've got to hold to a high degree the future rewards of patience over the short-lived pleasures of a moment. It is easy to overcome temptation if you keep your focus on the future. Let me tell this; if you are a person who is focused on the moment you are like a man of whom Sam Levenson speaks of; instead of praying that "Lead us not into temptations", the man prays saying "Lead us not into temptation", then adds to say "Just tell us where it is; we'll find it". Don't be such a one. Let me share with you an experience I had.

Halfway through Charlotte's pregnancy, we had gone to visit a family friend whose wife had traveled out of town.

As we relaxed over a meal, a young lady came in asking for a place to stay; she had just moved into town. My friend was reluctant to take her in in the absence of his wife, and so he turned her away. That evening when we returned home, Charlotte was concerned for the young lady and asked me if we could take her in. She became part of our family, and we treated her as Charlotte's young sister. Two months before the expected date of delivery Charlotte had to go to Mum's place for special attention as this was her first pregnancy. The young lady we gave shelter to, and I remained alone the whole period my wife was away.

A few weeks that followed, I would walk into the house only to find the girl stark naked, and with no apology or excuse, she would allow me to escape the scene. This happened on more than three occasions; I realized I was under attack. I started avoiding my own home. I would get home very late at night and leave very early in the morning to avoid being with her. I knew that if I allowed a suitable environment to be created, I would fall for her enticement. When my wife returned, I told her that the young lady we offered our shelter wanted more than housing. We diplomatically excused her without creating any public ridicule for her.

I learned my lesson, I could have taken the opportunity of the moment, but the future was speaking louder than the moment. I imagined the destiny ahead of me then I would imagine a sexual scandal following, I respect the future.

I was not going to forsake the future on account of a few

sexual encounters with this young lady. Ralph Waldo Emerson once said, "We gain the strength of the temptation we resist." Overcoming that one temptation gave me the strength to overcome future temptations of like manner.

The Surest Way to Protect Against Temptation

Joseph resisted, resisted and resisted and finally he fled. Resist the devil, and he will flee, but in this instance, Joseph is the one who fled. In the case of Joseph, Potiphar's wife could not escape because she owned the environment; hence, Joseph had to be the one to avoid. Imagine yourself in a brothel; please don't expect that the prostitute in that house will flee if you resist her because the environment empowers her to stay.

But what are you doing there in the first place? Like Joseph, you went there to do your housekeeping duties because you were assigned to work there that week. Flee from that place even if it means you were losing your job. Now imagine you are in Church, and you look at somebody, and the enemy wants your mind to dwell on that person leading you to lust. Will you walk out of a church? Resist, and the devil will flee from you. Some cases call for you to escape.

In the words of Mark Twain, "There are several good protections against temptation, but the surest is cowardice."

How valid those words are. You must be a coward in the face of temptation; coward not by giving in helplessly, but coward by running away from the temptation. Don't cheat yourself to be strong, run. I'm reminded of a friend who once worked in a chain store; he had learned how to steal without being caught. He had tried on many occasions to resist the temptation, but he found himself stealing. One day he just resolved to quit the job and find another which didn't require him to handle money directly. Running away is the surest way to protect yourself against temptations.

I will repeat this in concluding this section; in the face of temptation, the fear of the Lord is the only ultimate guard you've got. "There hath no temptation taken you but such as is common to man: but God is faithful, who will not suffer you to be tempted above that ye are able; but will with the temptation also make a way to escape, that ye may be able to bear it. Wherefore, my dearly beloved, flee from idolatry." 1 Corinthians 10:13.

God is faithful! That is the point I want to stress in this verse. You may ask; how is God faithful in the face of temptation. Firstly he will not allow you to be tempted beyond what you can overcome. Therefore every temptation that comes the way God has supplied to you the grace (ability) to overcome.

Secondly, He not only gives you the ability to overcome, but He also makes a way of escape.

In case you may ignore or otherwise remain unaware of the grace supplied to you. God goes further to cover that by providing a way of escape.

In the face of Temptation, God is faithful. Resist dream robbers and destroyers. Private sins may bring a public embarrassment. God gives people what I call the grace period. That is the period God allows you to work on yourself so that sin is rid of your life. God doesn't judge or punish you immediately; instead He gives you the grace period so that you can go and live as an overcomer.

"We sometimes confuse the feeling of temptation with that of giving in to temptation. The danger here is that sometimes, feeling that we have allowed ourselves to fall, we despair of ourselves and allow ourselves to fall further" – *Shraga Silverstein (A Candle by Day).*

CHAPTER NINE

MIND YOUR GARMENT

"The one who holds your garment tells the story"
– Andrew Mudolo

Martin Luther King, Jr. once said: "The true measure of a man is not how he behaves in moments of comfort and convenience, but how he stands at times of controversy and challenge." How do you deny an accusation when circumstances prove otherwise? How do you put up a defense when the evidence speaks against you? Joseph, as we have seen, was found in this kind of predicament and nothing he said could vindicate him of the allegations leveled against him. Are you a minister of the Gospel, a singer, a medical doctor, whoever you are, you have a garment that you should protect. Your garment is what gives you identity and ethical covering. Society expects a certain level of standards from different walks of life.

There is nothing as painful as the pain of suffering for something you never did. Sometimes people become careless, and they find themselves implicated in matters which they fail to exonerate themselves. Take, for example, into today's world of technology; people are so naïve about the emails, Twitter, and Facebook accounts. I have often gone to internet cafes only to find a previous' uses account open. In such cases what I do to educate the owner is that I'll send a message from their account to my own and then respond to it with information to help them mind the internet habits and practices. People go on the internet or use their mobile gadgets without any concern for digital footprints. If you are going online, please equip yourself with the necessary knowledge and software to help protect your garment.

A story is told of a man of God who at gunpoint was forced to undress and have sex with a woman hired for that purpose. When the man of God refused to have intercourse with the woman, he was made to lie down next to the woman, and the gunmen took photos of the couple. The man of God for fear of a scandal would pay the gunmen at their request several monies to avoid the public embarrassment. The gunmen had the man's garment, and they sure had a story.

In the period of writing this book, a great Bishop was sent to prison by the anti-corruption commission for bribery. The kind-hearted Bishop was helping an unemployed gentleman find a job at a local Council authority and introduced him to a senior officer.

On leaving the office of this council senior officer, the gentleman seeking employment remained behind and dropped an envelope with a substantial amount of cash.

The officer reported the act and the Bishop, together with the gentleman seeking employment were apprehended, charged, and sent to prison for the offense of bribery.

Many stories can be told, but one thing is for sure, if you are a man with a great destiny, take care of your garment. The enemy has set his eye on you and will continuously present before you opportunities for compromise. If he can't drag you into sin, he will go all-out to get hold of your garment for propaganda. Remember this point; whoever holds your garment tells the story. When people are presented with the obvious, no explanation will hold. When the enemy has cast eyes on you, he will not rest until he gets his way. It amazes me how often men of influence disregard the protection of their garments. Never take it lightly; one lie well-arranged can be the undoing of many efforts of several years of character and testimony building.

Before God, you stand innocent and that my dear reader is what is of paramount importance but never neglect the building of a right social image. Jesus grew and gained favor both with God and men. You have no control over how people see you, but you have a choice as to how you present yourself before men.

Joseph went about with his business as usual, and that is the case most times; you are preaching in a crusade or attending a meeting miles away from your home, and you pull out a pair of ladies lingerie on stage instead of a face towel.

What story will people say? You might be busy making promises as you go about your usual daily business, realize that those promises may be out on record and will in future be the evidence that seals your downfall.

The higher you go in the society, the more the eyes looking at you. Protect your garment.

Accusation Is Not Cessation

When a person holds your garment; they usually present an allegation against you. Allegations have the potential to impact the journey to your destiny diversely, but it can never alter the outcome of your destiny. It was alleged that Joseph wanted to rape his Master's wife; this angered Joseph's master who threw Joseph into the prison for this alleged attempt. Right there is potential for malice and bitterness; many would have given up on life and even on God. But for Joseph, his God was more to him than the gold he would have had in Potiphar's house.

If all you have is from God, then when you lose it, you'll never whine about it knowing that the same God is still in control. But alas many owe their present life to their efforts and hard work never seeing the hand of God hence the complaints when it is taken away.

It is often true that those whose case is weak make the most clamor.

When you are falsely accused, always remember the words of

Marcus Tullius Cicero. He said, "As fire when thrown into water is cooled down and put out, so also a false accusation when brought against a man of the purest and holiest character, boils over and is at once dissipated, and vanishes and threats of heaven and sea, himself standing unmoved."

One of the fights you will encounter as a person pursuing destiny is the battle of the mind; the enemy is continually reminding you of your past failures saying that you are not worthy of anything good in life. This will extinguish your passion for your dreams, and your efforts of hard work will turn into passivity.

These accusations from the enemy hinder your confidence in approaching your father with our request when he has said, call to me, and I will answer, ask and you shall receive, seek and you shall find, knock and the door shall be opened. So, "Cast not away, therefore, your confidence, which hath great recompense of reward. For ye have need of patience, that, after ye have done the will of God, ye might receive the promise".

There is another level of accusation which comes as a malicious sword from the mouth of those from whom you cut company. There comes a time on destiny journey where you leave Potiphar's house. There are friends whom you should cut from your circle.

Those who drag you into compromise are fellows you should put in your past. But be rest assured they will not stay silent.

They have a word to say about you, how that you think you are better than them.

Come to think of it when a person walks away from a circle of friends that lead them to compromise; the tendency is always to see the wrong in the person walking away.

Tell a person off to their face for their wrong, and you can be assured of them labeling you as a holier than thou. If you confront sin, you will be accused. It may mean a loss of employment on account of your denial of a corruption proposal. The accusation is always fashioned to put the blame on you, discredit your character, and integrate.

There is an exciting story of an American football player named Brian Banks. Brian allegedly dragged Wanneta Gibson into a stairway at the Polytechnic High School in Los Angeles and raped her there, said Miss. Wanneta.

Mr. Banks was sent to prison on account of the allegations. Wanneta also went on to sue the school and won millions in damages in the same case. This incident happened in 2002. In 2011 Wanneta contacted Banks and asked to meet up with him. Of course, Banks agreed. Banks was well prepared for the encounter; it is possible that Wanneta's conscious was torturing her. Wanneta confessed to fabricating the story. Unknown to her Banks was recording the whole confession. As fire when thrown into water is cooled down and put out, Bank's conviction was overturned in 2012.

Banks spent years in prison for a crime he didn't commit.

Believe me; there are many people like Joseph, young men like Banks who are serving sentences they know nothing about.

When you are falsely accused, you can choose to throw tantrums or let God vindicate you. The fact is that the truth will undoubtedly come out.

The accusation of men is trash when your innocence is before God. As long as God approves of you and your resistance to sin and injustice, any allegation against you is a waste of time and energy. The God that sees in secret will reward you openly. God sees the secrets of the heart and knows your motives and intentions; He will vindicate you. Be of great cheer the Lord is your defense. It was Israelmore Ayivor who said, "There is 100% assurance that what your friend's enemy tells you about your friend is false. What your failure tells you about your passion is fake."

Don't give up." It is time to go above and beyond false accusations.

"Malice scorned, puts out itself; but
argued, give a kind of credit to a false
accusation" – Philip Massinger

CHAPTER TEN

IMPRISONED MASSES

"You are never truly free until you are free to think" – Andrew Mudolo

---

A prison is never a place of comfort no matter the amenities provided. Being a prisoner is one of the most frustrating experiences, especially if you are innocent. A prisoner, also known as an inmate or detainee, is a person who is deprived of all liberty against his or her will. I can be by confinement, captivity, or by forcible restraint. The term applies particularly to those on trial or serving a prison sentence in prison." I know you may not be in any physical prison-like Joseph, but please allow me to speak to you. I have this saying that "the world of dreams and ideas is an ocean of infinity." There are endless ideas out there. When we thought the typewriter was an amazing idea along came the computer.

When we thought the idea telegram was the fastest way of

communication, along came the mobile phone era.

Yes, when we thought voice calling was the most significant thing, along came the era of video calling.

The World Of Dreams And Ideas Is An Ocean Of Infinity.

Being a prisoner implies that you are a person under restrictions and deprivation. Are you among the masses deprived of the liberty of mind; the freedom to think and dream big? Do you fill trapped in your current circumstances and make no effort of thinking of better ways? Have you resigned from efforts of improvement to change your life? You are never truly free until you are free to think. Many people believe they are free, but the truth is that they are under slavery – mental slavery. Billions of people are imprisoned into thinking what other people have said and projected to them. People have created systems of thought that are now governing the world. Let me give you an example. Until recently, people's thought paradigm was; go to school, get good grades and proceed to University. Graduate with honors and get Job. Marry, get a mortgage, and have children. Aspire for the top of the corporate ladder and make it big in retirement. Well, who said that that was the appropriate path of life for everyone? It is no longer a focus on one's passion instead, it is a pursuit of material substance. To be a dream achiever, you must move in life with deliberate thought. Are you living a mindless, thoughtless life? Endeavor by all means to carry your mind along as you journey in life.

Inability And Refusal To Think

I want to be deliberately blunt here and say that MOST PEOPLE DON'T THINK. Furthermore, when you engage their minds in an attempt to awake them to the fact that they don't think they refuse to believe. The Bible and many other writings confirm the fact that a man is his thoughts. In other words, you are what you think.

Remember, I'm talking about imprisoned masses; not those prisoners behind bars of iron but the millions of people behind mental bars. It was Henry Ford who said, "Thinking is the hardest work there is, which is probably the reason why so few engage in it." In Zambia, there is a popular excuse for refusal to engage in rigorous mental work – we say "Critical thinking can lead to insanity." Thinking is hard work. Unfortunately, many people are lazy, and that is why very few people think. The truth is this: thinkers rule the world. Those who think are few, that is why they appear like madmen to the rest of the people. Thus to change the world, one needs a certain degree of madness. Madness is, therefore in this sense, a state of being affected with a high degree of intellectual independence.

J. Churton Collins once said, "Half our mistakes in life arise from feeling where we ought to think, and thinking where we ought to feel." Most of life's decisions should be based on logic and not emotion. Many people tend to be emotional about life, and they suspend all forms of reasoning.

Life is more like a puzzle. If you sit and cry and get all emotional about the problem; it will forever remain a puzzle.

But the day you decide to approach a puzzle with logic, you will in time solve it. Life is like that. If you approach life with emotions, you'll end up with the same problems all the time. It is time to employ the wonder of logic and change the circumstances of your life.

Learn to think for yourself. Independent thinking is vital if you are to achieve your dream. If you refuse to think, other people will think you out of your dream. To be original, you must think original.

Don't be a carbon copy of other people. Yes, you can draw

strength from what other people have said and achieved, but still, that does not replace independence of thought. In the words of J. Firtzjames Stephen, he says, "Originality consists in thinking for yourself, and not in thinking, unlike other people." Learn and draw inspiration from the thoughts, works, and accomplishments of other people but still think for yourself. Sadly as Bertrand Russell affirms, "Most people would rather die than think; in fact, they do so." Friends to go above and beyond life's happenings, you must be a person who loves and enjoys the discipline of deliberate thought.

"If you think you are beaten, you are. If you think you dare not, you don't. If you'd like to win, but think you can't it's almost a cinch you won't. Life's battles don't always go to the strong or faster man, But soon or late the man who wins is the one who thinks he can" – Unknown

Take Care of Your Mind

It is said that all problems are knowledge problems and all solutions are knowledge solutions; thus if you are going to be a person of solutions, you must be a person of knowledge. Problems often signal a lack of knowledge. Acquiring knowledge is not easy because it requires your mind to do it.

"Nurture your mind with great thought, for you will never go any higher than you think" – Benjamin Disraeli.

Taking care of your mind entails nurturing it – feeding, developing, and empowering it with what is necessary for it to remain relevant. Do you know why you can't find solutions to some things happening in your life? You fail to find answers and solutions not because answers and solutions can't be found. The reason for the failure is that the answers and solutions exist outside of our knowledge-base. You see, answers and solutions are invisible to you because your mind is not developed enough for it to generate thoughts to reach and vibrate at the height of the question or problem.

Learn to invest in your mind. Your mind is the most significant assets your own, please take care of it. As relates to reaching your dreams and aspirations in life, there is one crucial thought discipline you should develop; that is creative thinking. As much as your purpose or dream is unique, it does not imply that it's the first of its kind. This is where creativity comes into play.

Take for example; two boys may have the dream of playing professional football and let us say they succeed. What will make one play celebrated over the other is how he employs the creative process. Allow me to share some tips that could help you develop your creativity:

1.   **Be a Learner**: The moment you stop learning, you stop growing and start dying. If you are going to be a creative thinker, you must be willing to learn. You must glean specific material directly related to your dream and then learn general material by becoming fascinated with a wide range of concepts. Let give you an example. You can study all materials related to football and still succeed but if you go an extra mile to learn about stress and how a person can reduce stress in their life; that might give you a creative edge. After learning about stress and how to overcome it, you can relate your knowledge to the way you play football so that your fans find it stress freeing watching you.

2.   **Be thorough**: Don't be bored by detail. To become a creative thinker, you need to love 'detail.' Most people miss a lot of opportunities because they don't pay attention to details. When you gather material for learning, make sure you are thorough in your understanding of the materials. One way you can achieve that is by digesting the contents in your mind. Take some time to focus your thoughts on the materials you've learned.

3.   **Retract**: It is essential once in a while to withdraw

from your materials and thought and engaged in something apart from it. Perhaps you could go hang out with your friends and let your mind flow in another direction while you enjoy yourself. Deep in your core, the material of focus is still being processed, and before you know it, your subconscious mind will begin to register creative ideas relating to your materials into your conscious mind.

4.   **Share to get feedback**: Share your ideas with other people and allow them to give you honest feedback. If you are going to go very far in achieving your dream, you must learn to appreciate and value feedback. If you don't have the money to get professional feedback on your ideas, you can rely on sincerer peer-to-peer feedback. Say your dream is to bring to the market unique bread. You can get feedback from your customers by first producing your bread at a small scale. That allows you to hear what your customers have to say before you can go to mass production. Feedback will allow for modifications to your dream, idea, or product.

According to psychology professor Barbara Kerr, "approximately 22 percent of the variance in creativity is due to the influence of genes". This discovery was made by studying the differences in creative thinking between sets of twins. If 22% of creativity is by the influence of genes, then the other 78% is creativity by way of learning and development. Therefore, it is a mistake to conclude as we often think that creativity as an event or a natural skill that some people have, and some don't. For a fact, research suggests that both creativity and non-creativity are learned. Friends, it is time to suspend all those claims and excuses of saying that "I'm just not the creative type." I don't deny that some people have a high propensity for creativity than others. However, nearly every person is born with some level of creative skill, and the majority of our creative thinking abilities are trainable. How could Joseph come up with the kind of solutions he came up to answer the challenge the king's dreams presented? How did Joseph build the storage house for the grain he bought? How did Joseph ensure efficient distribution of the grain in the time of famine? How did Joseph keep flawless account records for a national grain storage system? He did it all by CREATIVE THINKING.

Now you may be saying that you have freedom of thought and dream, very well. But take the time to analyze what drives your daily decisions and plans.

On average most individuals dream and make plans based

on what their income and savings can allow. This is the typical imprisonment that characterizes many people today. National governors, political leaders, businessmen and women, high school and university students alike suffer from this imprisonment.

If imagination is the greatest nation, then why do you allow your national boundaries to be your limitation? The fact that you are born in Africa or some disadvantaged environment does not make your imagination any lesser. If you dream, according to your present means and capabilities, you are a prisoner to be pitied.

One of the tragic experiences of prison is that you have no control over your life. The authorities plan everything you do; what time you sleep, what you eat, and what time you go to bed. This happens even to imprisoned dreamers. If others make your plans, dreams or aspirations, sorry, you are not free. I remember a story of a missionary imprisoned in Zambia who was forcibly accused of a grievous crime. In the term of his sentence, he wrote many books, and while in prison with help from his friends overseas he managed to publish his books. He received the books in prison and begun to give copies to some of the inmates with him. This missionary was free to think, and his ideas went beyond the walls and gates of his physical imprisonment. You may be physically free but mentally imprisoned; limited in thinking by your geographical position, academic or professional qualifications, or family background.

Ideas are the means through which potential is awakened, and ideas still are how potential is embodied. Potential is incarnate in your ideas, and as long as you are not thinking or imagining, your potential is far from being realized.

God gave you imagination ability so that you can transcend you present to allow you to see with the eyes of your mind the future your potential can achieve. Do you have singing, business, pastoral, athletic, corporate, or engineering potential? Please take time to use your imagination and see what your future looks like. The great thing about creativity is that it knows no limits. The only restriction on imagination is the one you impose on it. Presently you may not have the money to undertake your business ideas, but imagination will allow you to see into the future your business in full maturity. Let your mind travel to the future that your potential can create. When people are resigning to the popular dogma, you rise beyond that box and think for yourself. Thinking men rule the world; you have a choice to either be a thinker or a follower of other men's thinking. You must be strong if you are going to break those gates of mental imprisonment.

IT WON'T BE EASY, BUT IT CAN BE DONE!

Revolt from localized thinking and go into infinity to make withdraws of great possibilities.

CHAPTER ELEVEN

CREATING OPPORTUNITIES FOR YOUR DREAM

"People don't care how much you know until the know how much you care" – Theodore Roosevelt

---

Every day of your life, you are coming into contact with people of various sorts carrying with them different kinds of challenges and problems. Do you pass by at the sight of a motor accident? Do care enough to ask how the weekend was for your colleague at your workplace? Do you bother to find out whether that child playing with your son or daughter is in school? Society has so conditioned us to be numb to the feelings, pain, and problems of other people and focus on our own. We are conditioned to pass by with no reflection on the sorrow and suffering of those around us. Do you care enough to ask or find out?

"When Joseph came to them in the morning and looked at them, he saw that they were sad and depressed. So he asked Pharaoh's officers who were in custody with him in his master's house. Why do you look so dejected and sad today? Genesis 40: 6 – 7.

I believe this world would be a better place if we all employed Joseph's attitude towards others even when we are in the heat of the prison experience. Do you wonder why others are having solutions to the problems of the world around them? It's because they care enough to find out. The garbage or sewerage problem in your area should be a matter of concern to you. The poor performance and growth of our nation's economy should become your concern. Only when you make it a thing of your interest, can you appeal to your inner resources and potentials. There Pastors who are making no impact in their community because they decide not to get involved. Politicians, who are in oblivion all the term of their service awaiting the next election, why? The problems of their areas do not concern them. But you can do better; make it your concern. Anjezë Gonxhe Bojaxhiu popularly known as Mother Teresa cared enough about the impoverished masses of India to become the legend that we talk about today. The ability to be touched by the afflictions of others is the key that stirs up the unrealized potential to respond. No matter how numb society has conditioned you if you are to going to make any meaningful, lasting impact, you must be both sympathetic and empathetic. You should desire to be of help to others

Move away from the attitude of ignoring others. Men of old entertained angels by being hospitable to strangers let me share with you a little experience I had one time at work. I was at the office one afternoon.

As we were chatting with my workmates, an older man walked in and excused himself, wanting to be attended to.

I greeted him warmly and asked what I could do for him. He requested for the accountant. "Do you have an appointment," I asked. "No," he responded, explaining the nature of the business he followed. I then took him to the accountant's office. He appreciated my warm gesture and went on to meet with the accountant. Back at the office, one of my colleagues asked me if I knew the man. I didn't even have a clue who the man was; to me, he was just another customer that needed to be attended to. It happened that the old man was one of the richest men in our city whom I had just been hearing about. To my colleague, my warm greeting and manner in which I attended to the man suggested that I must have known who the man was. Well, for me, I treat people the same. Rich or poor, young or old; I warmly greet them and within my powers, help them.

Many great businesses were founded by those who made the lack of something or a problem their concern. Are you unhappy with the services you are receiving from your internet provided? Make it your concern. You are a teacher, is the poor performance of your pupils a concern? Are you are a politician, troubled about the welfare of your people in your constituency?

Is the level of corruption a concern to your heart? Unless you make it your interest, you are far from being the solution provider. You are far from becoming the "Joseph" of your generation or industry. You may have the gifts, talents, training, skills, and expertise required to offer the solution, but until you make it your concern, you are far from being helpful. Don't just be passive about the issues around you. We need men and women who are caring. We need leaders who are concern about the issues of countries and not just their pockets and families. We need clergymen who will offer themselves to the service of the people and not enthrone themselves as Lords over God's flock. Do you care enough to ask?

Givers Rule

One way you can create opportunities for your dream is by being a giver. "We hope to intensify philanthropy and encourage people to get started younger" this was said by Bill Gates. Before I dive into this giving business in detail, I would like to refute from the onset of a notion that has misled many people. When I say givers rule, I'm not talking about the common practice of the prosperity preachers. What I'm presenting to you in this chapter is not anything close to the practice of sowing money as a seed to your pastor in the hope of financial harvest. What I'm presenting to you is real life principles, not superstitious nonsense.

In 2010, Bill Gates, together with his wife Melinda, and Warren Buffet, came up with an initiative called Giving Pledge.

The Giving Pledge is a commitment by wealthy individuals and families to give away more than half their wealth to the causes of a better world – poverty alleviation, refugee aid, disaster relief, global health, education, women and girls' empowerment, medical research, arts and culture, criminal justice reform and environment sustainability. Let me share with you some excerpts from a few letters of billionaires who signed the pledge:

"It is my great pleasure to provide this Giving Pledge commitment wherein I pledge to give at least 50% of my wealth to charitable causes both during my present life and beyond. As a private

person, I prefer to minimize publicity of my philanthropic activities but at the same time realize that setting a positive example is the best way to encourage others to give back."
Leonard H. Ainsworth – Australia,

"From day one, my parents have been instrumental in instilling the ethos of philanthropy, particularly my responsibility as a Muslim to give and care for the less fortunate in our society.

"By signing this pledge, I hope to inspire my peers, fellow Africans and citizens of the world to take a close look at the funds they truly need to maintain their families versus their ability to give. In retrospect, many of us have well-above what we need while constantly accruing a list of what we want in this life. We all have a moral obligation as the more affluent in society to give back as best we know-how. I'll leave you with a few words I share with many of my comrades: 'When God blesses you financially, don't raise your standard of living. Raise your standard of giving."
Mohammed Dewji – Tanzania

"Let's create wealth through the diligent, pioneering, and innovative spirit of entrepreneurs, and share this wealth through the generous, selfless, and dedicated spirit of philanthropists. Let's make philanthropy a value, a faith, a commitment, and a lifestyle."
Dong Fangjun – China

"There is no greater privilege than to be fortunate enough to devote the majority of one's time and resources to helping others — to making our community, and the planet, better than we found it." Nick and Leslie Hanauer – United States

"The true measure of who we are and the ultimate fulfillment we can enjoy is based on how we share our gifts with the multitudes of our fellow human beings who live their lives without hope. Sharing our good fortune with others allows our legacy and purpose to become lasting and meaningful. Unconditional giving of ourselves, and what we have, reflects a nobility of spirit which reaches out and binds all of us." Dean and Marianne Metropoulos – United States

"Potential is no guarantee of progress. We will only grasp the staggering potential of our time if we create on-ramps that empower ALL people to participate, regardless of background, country of origin, religious practice, gender or color of skin." Robert Frederick Smith – United States

The giving pledge is a sure sign of how rich people are making efforts to contribute to the betterment of our world.

When people advocate for the Robinhood movement towards the rich; the rich realize their obligation to contribute to those less privileged. It is immoral to criminalize rich people for wealth legitimately acquired. For sure, you and I were destined to reign in life, and God desires that you reach that destiny. But don't just sit there and expect someone to give you handouts. Get up on your feet and see what you can do for others. Remember the Abrahamic covenant under which you are privileged to be a part of in Christ Jesus. It is an agreement where you are not only blessed, but your blessing translates into blessing others. You are blessed to be a blessing. From the signatories to the Giving Pledge you can sense a heart and mind that appreciates in practical terms the Abrahamic Covenant – BLESSED TO BE A BLESSING.

The World's wealthiest people are putting into reality what the Bible says we should do. Like Joseph, we can see that the GIFTS, TALENTS, MONEY, etc. should be used to the service of humankind. Joseph made sense of his destiny journey by dispensing his blessing (gift) for the benefit of other people. To appreciate the privilege of blessing, you MUST become a BLESSING.

In reading the story of Joseph, you should appreciate the fact that it did not matter the level which he found himself at, he always became successful. In Potiphar's house, he gave the best of his energy, time, talent, knowledge, wisdom, etc. and in his humble duties, he was noticed by his master and promoted.

In prison the same pattern is replicated, and it is no accident, Joseph had a flourishing relationship with God, He kept himself from sin, did all his work with diligence and full effort and interestingly he never charged for the interpretation of dreams. Imagine Joseph before the king of Egypt, saying, "King; this dream is quite something; what will be my reward?" Joseph could have charged the King handsomely, and for sure the king would have managed to pay. But if Joseph demanded payment, I'm fully persuaded he would not have been raised to the position of vice president of Egypt.

Instead of giving excuses for a rough childhood, the teenage abuse you suffered at the hands of your parents, you can go above and beyond it all to stun your abusers and those that envisioned your failure by a giving pledge. Give life all you've got, and it will give you all you can get. Be a giver of your gift to others, and the reward will come by Principle of reciprocal. Don't be a giver of excuses but a giver of your gift.

Givers rule; when you give, you inevitably position yourself for a receiving. Joseph's reward was determined after he released his gift as a service, not as merchandise. Why would Billionaires be giving away more than half of their wealth? Is it because they are expecting the world to pay their kindness with more billions?

Giving is only giving if you give to those that cannot give back to you. This is why the Bible and many other religious books always place the poor as a high priority for our help.

Be willing to offer your GIFT, MONEY, WISDOM, etc. for free, and when the benefit is realized, you will be surprised by the rewards you will receive. Have a giver mindset and not a receiver mindset. Let the only compensation you are looking to obtain, be the satisfaction of serving your gift to others. If you are looking for money as a reward for your gift, you will not reach your dreams because money has a way of eluding illegitimate seekers.

When people can't see the tangible benefit of your gift, they may undervalue it. This is why in specific fields like engineering the use of simulations and modeling is popular; it only saves to show the intangible tangible, so that valuation is accurate. I would like for you to settle this in your mind; GIVERS RULE!

Jim Carrey is probably the single highest paid comedic actor in the world and has been for some time now. But what most people don't know about him is that Jim Carrey comes from a very humble background. He grew up in a financially challenged family. Despite the poverty in the family Jim discovered his calling and was able to make sense out of his challenge.

He said that he developed his humor and funny antics while he was miserable because he needed to be funny to make his family smile when times were tough. The situation was terrible that at one point Jim dropped out of high school and he lived with his family in a VW bus at the time. The family would roam around Canada in the bus and live out of it. Finally, they ended up moving to his sister's house.

But not into their house, the family parked the VW bus in front and set up a tent on his sister's front yard. This was right before he decided to move to America and be a comedian. After a short stint doing stand-up, Carrey landed a role on the show In Living Color, and his career boomed from thereon. At Age 28, Jim had made an important discovery in his life. Serving his gift for free to his family helped him realize what he was born for. He said his purpose and life calling is using comedy to 'free people from concern.' It was his family background that led Jim to this discovery. Without any price, he was doing his best to put smiles on the faces of his family members. Just like Joseph; by offering his gift to Pharaoh little did he realize that he was saving his family from extinction. Jim was able to make sense out his childhood poverty – 'Free people from concern using comedy.'

You too, can make sense of the experiences of your life, both positive and negative. One way of achieving that is by offering your gift to the service of humanity. Whatever advantage and privilege you have in life; use it to help other people. By so doing, you will be solving the mystery of fulfillment in life.

Finally, you must avoid the temptation of serving others for your selfish benefit. When you help someone, don't go and publish your act in the streets. Let God be your witness. This is why I don't applaud churches or people that announce their acts of charity.

In a way, announced charity somewhat degrades the receiver. For the sake of the cameras, they may show a smile and occasional tears, but the damage to people's worth and self-esteem is grave. Jesus said when your right hand gives don't let your left hand know about it. I know that Jesus was using metaphoric language to talk emphasize the principle of right motive in giving. But we can still embrace the literal meaning of the act of giving being a secret. Giver rule! Resolve to be one today.

Givers rule! If you learn to serve others with your gift, talents, skills, abilities, and expertise; you will make sense of your destiny journey.

CHAPTER TWELVE

A DOSE OF DISAPPOINTMENT

If hope delayed makes the heart sick (see Proverbs 13:12), what happens to the core when hope is shattered and destroyed? The postponement of an awaited result can be very devastating. Imagine you are due for promotion and all indications point to the fact that you are the right man for the job. Then as you await a letter of appointment, you see a colleague of yours being congratulated.

How would you feel? From my many reading on the subject of disappointment, I have come to this conclusion – people commit suicide because of hopelessness which culminates into frustration.

When there is no sight of breakthrough or recovery from life's shocking events, suicide becomes the easy option. We all have expectations as we go on in life's journey and surely we expect the good.

If you're betrayed, release disappointment at once, it is serious cancer. You should strive in the face of offense never to let bitterness take root. When it comes to disappointment, if you persevere and learn from it, life has a way of compensating you in the process of life.

The Source of Disappoint

It is easy to blame other people for the disappointments of life. You see, disappointment is our response to the words and actions of other people. People are entitled to their own opinions, and there is nothing you can do about it. People's actions will result from their thinking, and there is nothing you can do about it. We suffer disappoint because of our expectations of people. If we expect kind words of praise, then they speak the opposite, you experience disappointment. Therefore disappointment comes from our expectations. In other words, when you consider a risky action, you form a prior expectation of the payoff, and if the outcome is worse than expected, you will experience an emotion called a disappointment. But if the result exceeds your expectation, you will feel happy.

> *"When you have expectations, you are setting yourself up for disappointment" – Ryan Reynolds*

Let me break it down for you: Life involves risks. Wisdom for life suggests that a person realizes that life itself is a risk. Everything that happens under the sun is a risk. When you fall in love, you risk your happiness, your freedom, etc. When you get a job, you risk, when you have children you risk.

Everything is a risk. Life is a risk because of the forces beyond our control. The weather can be a disappointment; say you plan a vacation.

And on the day of departure, as you are waiting in the departure lounge, you hear an announcement that your flight is canceled due to bad weather. That can be disappointing. Because life is a risk, you should expect the good, the bad, and the ugly.

When you speak, you risk being misunderstood.

When you love you risk being rejected.

When you ask you risk being denied.

When you run, you risk falling.

When you eat, you risk choking.

And when you do nothing, you risk everything.

The disappointment is more significant if the only thing you expect in life is good. When Jesus was preparing his disciples for his departure and eventual ministry, they'll have to carry out he did it well. Listen to the words of Jesus Christ in John 16: 33; "I've told you all this so that trusting me, you will be unshakable and assured, deeply at peace. In this godless world, you will continue to experience difficulties. But take heart! I've conquered the world" (MSG).

Here we see Jesus equipping His disciples for rough times; he also gives a consolation. He did not say to them, "guys, you have walked with me, the world will like you, and they will celebrate you everywhere you go."

He addressed their emotional intelligence; he prepared them for good, the bad and the ugly. Friends, today there is a false gospel that says you should never expect bad times in life.

Being positive does not mean only expect the good but positivity in life entails planning the bad too. You must mitigate the occurrence of adverse outcomes by doing your homework. So, if you marry, don't just go into it even when there are clear indications of abuse all in the name of expecting both good and bad.

Infinite Hope to Neutralize Finite Disappointment

Martin Luther King Jr. once said, "We must accept finite disappointment, but never lose infinite hope." Friends, I want you to appreciate the fact that disappointments are finite; they have an expiry date. They can happen, and you can go past them. You must learn to be in control and stop being a victim of disappointment. To overcome disappointment, one needs to have hope. Listen. When what we've been expecting is not realized, painful damage is inflicted on our hearts and emotions hence the need to master the art of overcoming disappointments.

We all have high expectations of ourselves, our family, church, employer, and they too are having expectations of us. Husbands expect their wives to be submissive while wives expect their husbands to be loving.

Parents are expecting their children to be respectful, and children are anticipating the parents to feed and educate them. We expect our governments to grow economies of our nations and the legislatures to enact democratic laws. Pastors have expectations of their flock, and the congregation has its array of expectations. And most importantly, God has expectations of his creatures, and the created also have expectations of their creator. It's good to hope and hold high expectations in all we do. Hope energizes you to attempt great things. In our relationships, we should hope, and it is that same hope that allows us to trust others.

What is hope? You may ask; Hope is an expectation of an outcome. Hope is the assurance that I am going to get something out of my labors and activities. Hope is the assurance of productivity. The only danger is that we live in a society that tells us only to expect the good. Listen to another passage, "But he said unto her, Thou speakest as one of the foolish women speaketh. What? Shall we receive good at the hand of God, and shall we not receive evil? In all this did not Job sin with his lips". Job could have been disappointed by God. How could a loving God allow this to happen to him? He could have said, "I have been faithfully saving him, is this the way he rewards me?"

I have shown you that the outcomes of life will either be good or bad. I have further established to you that disappointment happens when the result is not precisely what you were hoping for. I believe this is one thing most people have never emphasized in destiny journey.

Thomas Edison is quoted to have said: ***"I have not failed; I have just found 10,000 ways that won't work."***

What prompted Thomas Edison to try so many times to get it right finally? He knew that the outcome could either be good or bad. This knowledge is what he needed to motivate him to try again. Most people give up due to disappointment when they encounter a terrible result in their endeavors.

If today you get disappointed, try again and again and again until you succeed.

It is Edison who also said, "Many of life's failures are people who did not realize how close they were to success when they gave up." It would appear to me that Edison's success came from a rich knowledge of life. He knew what to expect in life and knew how to manage the disappointments as he went along the journey to purpose.

Life has opportunities for disappointments, but you need to master the outcomes of every step you take; thus, you will avoid the acid of disappointment.

Joseph was presented with this opportunity; "But [even after all that] the chief butler gave no thought to Joseph, but forgot [all about] him (AMP). Genesis 40:23.

Joseph's request to his friend; who he had just helped tremendously forgot about him. I'm sure as the days went by in prison, Joseph could have significantly felt disappointed.

You must be brave about your relationship with God. Never allow the storms of life to lead you to a casual walk with God. With God on your side, you will make it to your land of hope. Like Joseph, you might have been forgotten, but God has not forgotten about you. Every trace of disappointment in your life will turn into divine appointment if you only look to God. Joseph walked with God, even though a man forgot him, God remembered him.

Because life has its ups and downs, you've got to prepare for both. When you hit the lows; don't let disappointment get the best of you instead master the "lows" and climb back up again. When it comes to fulfilling your dreams; there is no easy way. If you can't handle disappointment, it's most likely you won't see your dream through to accomplishment.From what I have already established, disappointment is almost unavoidable as long as you are alive, but if you learn to benefit from the disappointment, you can use it as leverage to even grow into your success.

As I conclude this chapter, allow me to ask you an important question; should you stop expecting good outcomes to avoid disappointment? Please don't miss this segment; it's what drives the point home. The key is this; do all you can, everything humanly possible to ensure a good, positive outcome but give room for the unexpected. When it comes to action, make sure you leave no stone unturned in preparation. Leaving room for the unexpected prepares you emotionally and psychological in case of a disappointing result.

Let me give an analogy of how to prepare for disappointment. In the rain season, everyone arms themselves with an umbrella, or a raincoat.

Almost now and then, before leaving our homes, we tune into the weather forecast to get an expert's daily analysis. Based on expert knowledge and our observations, we either carry the umbrella or leave it behind. The chances that you'll get socked during the season are minimized. But on the other hand, imagine a friend of yours pays no attention to the season, he does not prepare the tools required to protect himself and gives no regard to expert analysis.

Your friend is likely to get socked very often through the season. Firstly, Life, like the rainy season, has sunny days and rainy days. It would be a folly of you to be surprised that it rains in the rain season. In the same manner, it is folly to be surprised when you encounter disappointment in life.

Secondly, carrying your umbrella is like an emotional fortification; it shows readiness for whatever may come. You have not left it to chance, and you are prepared. Joyce Meyer says, "Depression begins with disappointment. When disappointment festers in our soul, it leads to discouragements".

Joyce makes a significant observation here. The quickest way to depression is for you to allow disappointment. Watch out; when things don't go the way you hoped they would; gather your pieces and move on. Don't create a museum around disappointment. And in the words of Thomas S. Monson; the principle of living significantly include the capacity to face trouble with courage, disappointment with cheerfulness, and trial with humility.

> *"If we will be quiet and ready enough, we shall find compensation in every disappointment."–*
> *Henry David Thoreau*

CHAPTER THIRTEEN

THE TURN OF SEASONS REQUIRE PREPARATION FOR OPPORTUNITIES

"To everything, there is a season, and a time to every purpose under heaven" – Bible

Nothing is permanent except nothing, times change and season change. To everything, there is a season. There was a season of rejection, accusation, and imprisonment in the life of Joseph with a few scores of success. And as sure as the harsh seasons, so sure was the season of joy, happiness, and lasting success. There is a time for weeping and a time for rejoicing; "Weeping may endure for a night, but joy cometh in the morning Psalm 30:5. When seasons change, they present new opportunities. When you sit in darkness for a long time, your eyes adjust, and soon you begin to find your way around quite easily. If you are not careful, you will get comfortable in the darkness, thinking that's all that is there for you. You should never be in the class of millions who have resigned all hopes of a change in circumstances. Things change, and seasons turn. With every sunrise, I have learned to see that it presents a shift. The darkness of a passing season cannot withstand the radiance and brilliance of the dawning season. You should always move in life with that assurance; things change and seasons turn.

Looking at the life of Joseph, we see that he suffered bitter rejection, a grave accusation, and was forgotten by the cupbearer, but God never forgot about him. You may be thinking the people that owe you favors have forgotten about you and for sure they might have. God is the one to appoint your change of season. God caused Pharaoh to dream, and Pharaoh commanded the change of season for Joseph.

When the season changes, your status changes, your companions change, and for sure your appearance never remains the same. When seasons change you too must change to suit the new season. That's where preparation comes into play. The turn of seasons is a critical time; you may be trapped in the passing season and fail to get a hold of the new season. Joseph realized this was his moment. He was not about to let the chance pass him by. He prepared to meet the king. When season change you've got to prepare. If you are not ready, you risk losing the opportunity coming to you as a result of a change in season.

Never hold on to a passing season as the relevance of certain things in your past season may be the very things that hinder your excellence in the new season. Always be hopeful, things must and inevitably will change in your life.

Jesus is our hope in this world of hopelessness. What season are you in currently? Trust the Lord for a turn of the season. God will make all things beautiful for you in the turn of the season. Weeping may endure for a night, but rejoicing comes in the morning.

Look ahead with great anticipation for a change in seasons for your life. I'm reminded of the words of William Arthur Ward, who once said: "The pessimist complains about the wind; the optimist expects it to change; the realist adjusts the sails." To make good of the changing season, you need to be a realist. Being optimistic is good, but optimism alone is not enough – action is a must. You can choose to complain about the way things are, or you can choose to be an optimist and live your life by chance. Better join the clique of realists; men and women, boys and girls who take life into their own hands and fashion out of it a future they imagined. Let us go on to look at how we can exploit opportunities.

"The best preparation for tomorrow is doing your best today" – H. Jackson Brown, Jr.

Change: Preparing For Opportunities

Everyone desires and keeps hoping that one day, their dreams will come to pass. But it is good to be real about things; Success demands a lot on your part. Colin Powell has conclusively identified the ingredients required for success; preparation, hard work, and learning from failure.

Powell says "There are no secrets to success. It is the result of preparation, hard work, and learning from failure.

Jim Rohn said, "You must take personal responsibility. You cannot change the circumstances, the seasons, or the wind, but you can change yourself. That is something you have charge of."

The most critical word in the process of preparation is change. Change is inevitable. You like it or not; life demands that you are continually changing. When it comes to change, you don't have to be stiff-necked. Work hard to change things in your life, but in certain instances, it is wise to change your attitude despite the things surrounding you.

Maya Angelou said, "If you don't like something, change it. If you can't change it, change your attitude".   There are things you will manage to change through hard work, and then other things you will need to go through them with a positive attitude. In the story of the 3 Hebrew boys, their convictions were that God would save them from the fire, but in case he didn't, they were prepared to face the fire (See Daniel 3). If you change things, you avoid being thrown into the fire. But should you be thrown into the fire, be brave enough to face the inferno.

What you require to face the fire is a change in attitude. Don't complain about the challenge; instead, change your attitude. The readiness to change is what allows one to embrace preparation. Preparation may involve discomfort to a degree. How certain it is that those who cannot change their minds cannot change anything. There can never be any progress without change; progress is impossible without change. I want us to refocus on the trinity I early presented on Preparation, Hard work, and learning from failure:

Do want to take hold of opportunities for great relationships, or perhaps for financial success?

Then you need to know and effectively practice the Trinity of Success: Preparation, Hard work, and learning from failure.

1.   **Preparation**: Involves putting everything in place that you will require in attaining your dream. Planning and budgeting are vital components in preparation, never shovel them away. Increasing your knowledge base, building capacity, and sharpening your skills are also part of preparation.

2.   **Hard Work**: Hard work is not manual, laborious work, and for sure, it is not mental, lazing around kind of work. Hard work is both physical and mental. To make your dream come true, it will not be a function of magic but a function of sweat, determination, and hard work. Vince Lombardi said, "The price of success is hard work, dedication to the job at hand, and the determination that whether we win or lose, we have applied the best of ourselves to the task at hand."

3.   **Learning from failure**: Here is a teacher who most people dislike even though they are ever inviting him – Failure. To fail means to miss the mark. Once, twice, a third and a fourth time and many more, you may miss the mark but don't lose sight of the fact that you've been getting better along the way. Winston Churchill once said, "Success consists of going failure to failure without loss of enthusiasm." Failure is just another stepping stone to greatness;

therefore, learn and keep learning from every failure. You will come out stronger.

Joseph was summoned from the prison by the most powerful man on the earth at that time.

He could have thought to himself, what I have I done this time around? Appearing before the King was no simple matter; a person had to prepare for an encounter with the King.

The king needed the gift Joseph had, but that was no excuse for dismissing Joseph's need for preparation. Joseph had to prepare himself.

"Then Pharaoh sent and called Joseph, and they brought him hastily out of the dungeon: and he shaved himself and changed his raiment, and came in unto Pharaoh." Genesis 41:14.

Opportunities abound in this world. No matter the urgency of need of your gift, lack of preparation is inexcusable. Joseph had to prepare himself and thanks to those who knew what the required preparation was.

Firstly shave your Head; The Israelites used to keep hair while the Egyptians kept no hair. Imagine Joseph from prison with his long hair going to appear before a hairless head, King Pharaoh. That would have in precise terms spelled disrespect and arrogance, hence the need for a shaved head. Joseph had to appear before Pharaoh, looking like an Egyptian. That's what preparation did for Joseph; it made him acceptable to the person who had the power to promote or demote him. You may find dear reader that you also need to shave your head – not literally, of course. If an opportunity comes your way, you need to shave off all thinking that may alienate you in the face of opportunity. Work on your knowledge base and bring it to the level of the opportunity presented to you. If the opportunity before you is engineering don't think or speak medicine; shave your head. Don't be rigid to change but be swift to adapt.

Secondly, Joseph needed to change your clothes; get rid of those prison rugs and appear in the right and acceptable attire. Joseph had to adorn himself and remove any trace of prison unpleasantness. One of the things you will have to overcome to be ready to take opportunities is an inferiority complex.

Build your self-esteem and confidence when faced with an opportunity. Building self-esteem stems from an awareness of your true self. If you see yourself as not being able, then you will probably miss the opportunity. If you don't value yourself, men will reevaluate your worth and consequently respond and take you according to the reevaluated worth.

No matter your location if you have the gift, the problem will seek you out. "I returned and saw under the sun, that the race is not to the swift, nor the battle to the strong, neither yet bread to the wise, nor yet riches to men of understanding, nor yet favor to men of skill; but time and chance happeneth to them all. For man also knoweth not his time: as the fishes that are taken in an evil net, and as the birds that are caught in the snare; so are the sons of men snared in an evil time, when it falleth suddenly upon them". You see, friends, God has leveled the playing field of life; "chance happens to them all." Opportunity knows no national, tribal, social status. An opportunity presents itself to all in the fullness of time. Joseph did not facilitate this opportunity, but his gift testified of him. Remember, givers, rule. Joseph had given his gift for service to his fellow prisoners was positioned to receive. What he received was an opportunity to change his life.

Opportunities abound for all, yet the opportunity is not enough as an opportunity. Opportunity is simply a door that you must walk through and not a destination where you stop.

Just as abundant as the opportunities are, so are the possibilities of missing them. Most opportunities are lost due to a lack of preparation.

The opportunity will not announce its coming. Therefore, you must always be prepared for the next level. Recognize your current position and then envision your next level then you will be informed of what preparation you must do to maximize the appearance of an opportunity.

I would love to give you my definition of preparation. Preparation is "pairing resources with demands in advance." So, to prepare for an opportunity, I suggest the following:

• **Identify your present**: The first and most important thing to do in the preparation process is the identification of the present in relation to your dream. Have an accurate and honest evaluation of where you are at present. If you ignore the present, the future will not welcome you. In looking at your present, avoid the temptation of only looking at what you could have been but also look at who you have become.

•   **Take an inventory of your resources:** Start by looking at what gifts God has given you. Your body, mind, voice, etc. are great resources that you can itemize. Clearly, outline what you have in your possession that would be of value or that you can use to bring profit. That is the first step to accurate preparation; Personal resource inventory.

•   **Identify your next step**: What is your immediate action in the direction of your dream? If you attempt to achieve the tenth step before making the second step, you will crash, and the crash may be irrecoverable. If you fail to pinpoint your tomorrow (the next step), it will be tough for you to step out with confidence. From my research, most things that are done without confidence seldom succeeds. Confidence will come from being sure of your next step.

Seasons will turn, opportunities will arise, but only those who are prepared will take advantage of the changes and gain the benefits. Therefore, it is of necessity that you prepare for your dream no matter what stage of life it is. Like the boys, Scout motto resounds. BE PREPARED!

No matter the urgency of need of your gift, lack of preparation is inexcusable.

CHAPTER FOURTEEN

GAINING WISDOM

Without Wisdom, efforts are misguided, gifts are limited, and without wisdom, opportunities are wasted. You need understanding as you journey to your destiny. "And Pharaoh said unto his servants, Can we find such a one as this is, a man in whom the Spirit of God is?" Genesis 41: 38.

"I said, Days should speak, and a multitude of years should teach wisdom. But there is a spirit in man: and the inspiration of the Almighty giveth them understanding. Great men are not always wise: neither do the aged understand judgment." Job 32: 7 – 9.

No matter your abilities, you need wisdom. Wisdom is paramount. Pharaoh understood one thing that most employers miss in today's engagements. "A man in whom the spirit of God is." Knowledge is a prerequisite if you are going to make sense out of your destiny journey.

To navigate the twist and turns on your journey to destiny, one must carry wisdom for a companion. In this chapter, I want to emphasize the importance of wisdom. To highlight the importance of wisdom allow me to look at several quotes by my mentor; Dr. Sunday Adelaja:

1.   **"If you have wisdom, you will be able to reign in every area of your life"**: To take and be in charge of your life in the land of your purpose requires wisdom. Thus any attempt to take charge and reign (excel and success) in any field of life without knowledge ends in embracement and disgrace; go for wisdom.

2.   **"Wisdom justifies a person in the face of any opposition"**: As I have already alluded to early, in the pursuit of your dreams, you will encounter opposition. When faced with opposition wisdom must answer that opposition. If you encounter resistance with ignorance and arrogance, the resistance is likely to break you. Wisdom will defend and speak for you. You will be justified by wisdom.

3.   **"If a person has wisdom, then he will also have the anointing. But sometimes a person with the anointing may not have much wisdom"**: Now here is a personal favorite. Many people are looking for energy and power to enable them to actualize their dreams. Unfortunately, they forsake wisdom to the peril. If you get wisdom, the same wisdom will also get you the energy and power you require. Ironically, people do everything to get the anointing (energy and power) then they are embarrassed because they apply the anointing without wisdom for catastrophic results. In all your getting, get wisdom!

4.   **"The foundational stone for any business, enterprise or project has to be wisdom"**: The dream you have for a business, successful career, education, healthy or financial future depends on wisdom. Wisdom is the bedrock on which all your dreams will be launched and sustained. Don't start building your dreams on the sand of ignorance; wisdom demands that you build on the bedrock of knowledge.

False Wisdom

Many have fallen into a mistaken belief that experience is wisdom. Wisdom is not gray hair; it goes beyond the whiteheads. Africa has some of the oldest Presidents ever, and if wisdom came by age, then Africa should have been a leading economy, a disease-free continent, and Africa should have been like Eden. Civil wars for decades, poverty of the highest extreme has characterized Africa, these are but a few of the many signs of the lack of wisdom.

The fallacy is that by old age the elderly have seen a lot of issues, appreciated these circumstances, learned a lesson and can give correct council in several matters. While this is true to some extent, when we subject this theory to some thought, we discover that experience is not sufficient for wisdom.

Experience is dependent on the environment an individual is exposed to and a host of other factors that are not constant from place to place.

One's experience in the North Pole may prove irrelevant to challenges and life of the Sahara desert. Experience is subjective, but wisdom is not, it is constant.

All manner of qualifications can never give wisdom. It is to be sought after like precious jewels. The price of wisdom is above gold and silver. It is better than weapons in a time of conflict. Wisdom is farfetched. I know you may be asking where then and how can one obtain it?

How wisdom comes

"There is a spirit in man". Wisdom springs from a regenerated spirit man. The spirit of man is not the source per se; God is. God is the giver of wisdom. "If any of you lack wisdom, let him ask of

God, that giveth to all men liberally, and upbraideth not; and it shall be given him." James 1: 5. In answer to prayer for wisdom, God pours His resources into the spirit of a man. The man must dig out the wells of wisdom within his spirit. That's the part where learning and experience come into play. Life's experiences, learning, and all manner of education endeavors strengthen one's access to that well of wisdom deep in the inside.

The next time you interview a candidate for an opening in your business don't forget the grand question, "Can we find such a one as this is, a man in whom the Spirit of God is."

This is the question Pharaoh asked. This is the wisdom question. When Joseph opened his mouth, Pharaoh identified a rareness of wisdom that surpassed all his sorcerers and magicians in all the land of Egypt. Beyond all his wise men, Pharaoh saw the wisdom of the divine in human clay in the person of young Joseph. Your earnest prayer must be for wisdom, ask God who gives without finding fault. The soberness of thought here is that wisdom will not come into you through some process of fusion or magical experience. Wisdom is to be drawn out from the inside of you. You can achieve this by learning and adequately appropriating your life's experiences.

"Wherefore be ye not unwise, but understanding what the will of the Lord is." Ephesians 5: 17. A lack of understanding of God's will is a folly. Therefore wisdom entails an understanding of the Word of God, which is an expression of God's will in written form. "When anyone heareth the word of the kingdom, and understandeth it not, then cometh the wicked one, and catcheth away that which was sown in his heart. This is he which received seed by the wayside." "And every one that heareth these sayings of mine, and doeth them not, shall be likened unto a foolish man, which built his house upon the sand:" Matthew 7: 26.

The ability to apply or practice the Word comes from a sound understanding of the scriptures. So, any individual void of a good knowledge of the scriptures is no candidate for the wisdom award.

Go for the Word, and you will surely gain wisdom. Joseph experienced betrayal and rejection in his early life. If experience was the only source of his wisdom, just imagine what kind of wisdom betrayal and rejection would produce if one fails to make sense out of it.

If you combine all of Joseph's experience, the outcome would be a ruthless, heartless tyrant beyond the worst of Pharaohs ever to live. It is making sense of his journey in the whole equation that neutralizes the acidic poisons of Joseph's experience to give him a heart that even his brothers could not believe but only stand dumbfounded.

When our life experiences are given to God, He gives grace for you to understand the high value of affliction.

This vast understanding produces the fruit of forgiveness.

Wisdom will only come to you, and if we give credence to the one whom all souls depend for their existence, the Almighty God.

"Seek knowledge, getting as much of it as you can and meditate on it; then you will become a happy possessor of wisdom" – Sunday Adelaja

CHAPTER FIFTEEN

UNDERSTANDING THE GIFT IN YOUR HAND

"A man's gift maketh room for him and bringeth him before great men" – Bible

Joseph possessed a rare gift, just like you and me. We all come to this world loaded with gifts, talents, and abilities. You too have a unique gift which is a means of realizing your dreams. You cannot achieve your dreams riding on someone else's gift. If you succeed riding on someone's gift, it's most likely the success, you achieve will be another man's success, the dream you realize may be another man's dream. Others are just there to complement and sharpen our gifts.

If the gift is critical to reaching your dreams, then this chapter serves to help you understand the gift variable in dream realization. Firstly, I'm going to be using the word gift and talent with some liberality as being interchangeable. Think of something you love doing, which makes people happy and has the potential of being your livelihood.

Thus, a gift is an endowment you possess at no cost and in essence, when you employ and deploy has the potential of being a blessing to others. It is a gift because nature gives it to you but yet carries with it a moral obligation of it being dispensed.

> ***Vocation is the place where our deep gladness meets the world's deep need – Frederick Buechner***

These gifts, talents, and abilities must be discovered, developed, and put into meaningful usage if they are to be of any help in your journey to your God-given dreams. Power untapped is as useless as powerlessness. The tools you need to take your dreams from remaining mare imaginations are the gifts, talents, and abilities that lay abundantly in you, sufficient for the journey.

The first difficulty people encounter is dream identification. Many people are multi-talented, multi-gifted, and multi-skilled, and that makes it challenging to settle on what to pursue. Briefly, let me highlight several ways of gift identification:

• **What are your Predispositions**: By way of creation you have a predisposition towards certain things and not others. You may tend to mental work like reading or a propensity towards emotions like empathy. Identify what comes naturally to you. I have learned in my personal life that I tend to read and help other people. Being able to identify these two trends has helped me to identify my gift of teaching.

• **What do you enjoy doing**: You have to discover what brings you great satisfaction. I believe that it is not hard to discover. You feel happy doing something that is engaging your gift, talent, and ability. I remember always being pushed to be goalkeeper playing soccer in my school days; it used to be a struggle. But when I did martial arts after high school, I enjoyed it.

Anytime was training time, I endure long hours of painful, rigorous exercises but enjoyed it regardless. I later enjoyed teaching martial arts to several groups in a day. It brought me great satisfaction and happiness. What makes you happy?

• **What is the testimony of others**: You cannot have a predisposition or engage in a gift of your great happiness, satisfaction, and not be noticed by careful observers. Friends and family can be constructive in helping you discover your gifts. Ask others to evaluate your tendencies and passions.

• **Revisit your childhood**: Children have the purest of dreams. They try out many things just for the fun of it. Those early years can point to great talent and potential. This is why I say every parent has a responsibility to provide an environment that supports their child's dream and purpose but never to impose dreams on them. You may see their gifts and fully understand your child's destiny, but you've got to let them discover it; provide the environment and pointers. Dr. Sunday Adelaja says, "In your journey to fulfill your purpose, you will hear deceitful voices." The saddest thing is when that deceitful voice is a parent's voice. Yes, you want your child to turn out a success, but it has to be their success, not yours. Let your child live his/her dream and never force your own on them. Your child's purpose is not hereditary; let them LIVE, give them FREEDOM TO BECOME.

• **Develop your strength**: It is possible to cultivate healthy character treats, but the truth is that each person has a point or area of strength. We all have strengths and weakness. If you focus on developing your strength, you will discover that they are all pointers to your core gift. Friends, your strengths are critical pointers that you should not ignore. If I may ask; do have a comprehensive knowledge of your gifts and talents? You should strive to turn your strength into a daily habit. Make sure you have a regular activity that empowers your discovered strength.

Apply effort: Winston Churchill once said; "Continuous effort, not strength or intelligence is the key to unlocking our potential. Here is another crucial point in discovering your gift and talent. As much as gifts and talents almost all the time flow out of a person naturally, there is a need for effort. You might be gifted, but if you lack energy, you may think it is not in you. Instead of jumping from one thing to another, settle on one to three at a time and ensure that you give it all your best. If it is not in you, you will know after a while of effort engagement. The effort is one thing that people don't see as being cardinal in discovering their talent or gift. You see, the principle of life is that nothing moves or changes unless some effort (force) is applied.

Reasons For Failure

The reason for failure to realize your dreams is not the lack of a gift, talent, or ability but a failure to develop and grow them.

It is a Principle of life that "all living things must grow." When there is no growth, death is the state of being. If your gift is not growing, it is dying. The gift has always been in your possession, but you have a responsibility to grow it. Nurture your gift through usage. The best way to improve your gift is to begin to use it. If you fail to reach your dreams, it's because you have been unable to grow or develop your gift. What should you know about people's failure to realize and utilize their gift? Firstly, you must understand that all men are born with a unique gift, the use of which gives excellent individual satisfaction and a sense of meaning in life.

Secondly, you need to understand that just like you; a gift is in infancy when you are born. Thus the gift must be fed, nurtured, and taken care of so that it can grow. Therefore a gift not developed continues to exist as an infant and is incapable of being used profitably. Thirdly, I want you to understand that a gift is not a guarantee of a successful life. It is not the gift pay say that brings you to greatness and purpose instead; it is the employment or deployment of it that culminates into success.

I trust you will do better. Imagine you possess a weapon of mass destruction, but you have no idea of how to lunch it. The weapon will be of no use to you; you'd be better off throwing it away.

Your gift is a weapon against poverty, sickness, mediocrity, racism, hunger, war, earthquake, global warming, etc. But if you remain ignorant of your gift, this world will continue to be ravaged by problems you were born to solve. Perhaps you know what your gift is; please don't end there, commit to developing it.

Set goals for your gift and make daily routines and activities that will cause your gift to be provoked to expand. And then don't forget to deploy it. Engage your gift for the benefit people around you.

Unless You Interpret A Dream, You Will Die In Prison.

What opened Joseph to the opportunity of leaving the prison were the dreams he had interpreted to the baker and the cupbearer. When Joseph made use of his gift, he secured his release. He used his gifts to help others, and his gift opened room for him to appear before the King. You will die in prison until you interpret a dream. If Joseph ignored his friends and withheld the blessing of his gift from them, he would have just closed the door; he would need to walk through, later. You will die poor until you interpret a dream, beloved unless you interpret a dream you will live a miserable life in the prison of poverty, mediocrity, insignificance, etc.

In the world of high unemployment rate, you will die jobless until you interpret a dream. In a society full of corruption, unless you interpret a dream, you will remain stranded. You will always be cut off from opportunities for elevation until you interpret a dream.

Sorry, but you will continue struggling in business never breaking through into profitability until you interpret a dream. Interpreting a dream is Joseph using his gift. In other words, what I am saying is this; Joseph's gift was that of interpreting dreams. Until he interpreted a dream, did he set his gift into motion. The gift you have must be dispensed. Interestingly the Bible doesn't seem to highlight prayer as the reason for Joseph's release from prison.

For argument's sake, let us say Joseph used to pray, crying to God day and night about the injustice of his imprisonment, would it not be logical for the scriptures to highlight to us. Joseph was a "Religious" man, but we don't see any Joseph wrestling with an angel-like Jacob. One thing I like about Joseph's story is the naturalistic flow of his life. Unlike Jacob, Joseph didn't have a wrestling fight with Jehovah. Unlike Moses, Joseph didn't encounter a phenomenon like the burning bush. Joseph's life does not spark with supernatural encounters. There is no dramatic shutting of Lions' mouths or the appearance of a fourth man. There is neither the militancy of Jehu nor the charisma of Elijah. Where is the miracle in a spoiled shepherd boy betrayed and sold into slavery by his brothers? Where are the miracle in slave work, accusation, and imprisonment?

Unfortunately, most people today think the journey of life must be punctuated with miracles; Friends a life of purpose does not necessarily have to be theatrical.

The journey of purpose may seem like ordinary life, but in time you soon discover that the miracle was the life itself and not the events in life. Have you ever paused to think through how far you come to be where you are today? Don't feel any less about who you are. Sometimes, people get too hard on themselves, thinking if they pray hard, fast more often or read the bible cover to cover.

Don't misunderstand me here; all those Christians rudiments are essential for a stable walk with God. The point here is that people do too much in the hope of adding some drama (miracles) to their lives.

A life of purpose may appear too miracle-less like that of Joseph. What is interesting to note is that Joseph's life is what is used to template a life of purpose.

Don't wait for an angel or some form of spectacular, out of this world experience to discover, live, and fulfill your purpose. Like Joseph go about blessing people with your gift. I can assure you that if you go about living everyday life, you will soon discover that the miracle is life itself and not the events in your life!

How do you interpret a dream?

Around you are dreamers; people with dreams of a corruption-free nation, a sound education system, a multi-billion corporation, an HIV/AIDS-free country.

Around you are dreams of various philanthropies to hurting

humanity. All these dreams are waiting for interpreters. You are interpreting a dream when you offer a service or product that solves a problem.

The problem is that people dream, but they fail short of the means to bring their dreams to pass. Dreamers are looking for interpreters. To interpret dreams implies that you become the channel that transmits the means through which another person's dream can be facilitated.

The truth is that there are people out there with great ideas, but without money to facilitate them and there are still many other people with money but without ideas. It is not accidental – Those with ideas must humble themselves to seek the partnership of those with the funds. And on the other hand, those with money must be humble enough to fund those with ideas.

The Gift Is Not For You

One of the most critical principles to understand is that the gift is not for you to use on yourself.

It is for service to humanity; the gift is the fruit you possess to give to humanity. If your gift is not helping others, sorry but you are not creating opportunities for it to bring you into your dreams. Unless you interpret a dream, you will die in prison; by that I mean you will live a frustrated life without a sense of purpose and fulfillment. To go above and beyond life's predicaments, you need to understand the importance of your gift, therefore, don't hold back effort; work towards making your dream a reality.

CHAPTER SIXTEEN

CELEBRATING UNIQUENESS

"Uniqueness is what sponsors identity and kills choice" – Andrew Mudolo

Let me open this chapter with the words of Linda Thompson; "Our uniqueness, our individuality, and our life experience mold us into fascinating beings. I hope we can embrace that. I pray we may all challenge ourselves to delve into the deepest resources of our hearts to cultivate an atmosphere of understanding, acceptance, tolerance, and compassion."

We are all in this life together." Our uniqueness should never be an occasion for discord and arrogant pride. Instead, it should grant us the sobriety of accepting and understanding other people's differences.

You may be wondering what I mean by uniqueness, let me give a working definition of uniqueness intrinsic for this book.

Uniqueness is the state of possessing characteristics and qualities that make a person stand out from the rest.

By implication, uniqueness is that "something" that makes you different from any other person.

Thus two people could be born at the same time, same time, from the same women but still be different. They may look alike, but there will be some quality that will make one stand out from the other.

People can identify you because you are a unique human being among many in this world. God created you my reader not only with a unique face and DNA but also with a gift and destiny that only you can fulfill. Your uniqueness is your key to being noticed; if you appear to be like another person, you can never be better than that person. Imitators never excel to the level of the ones they imitate or put another way; the one being mirrored always remains better than the imitator. Imitation is cheap, be yourself and reveal the rare uniqueness with which you were created. Egypt had many wise men, but only Joseph fit the position that arose because of the challenge that would before the land.

If what you want is orange when it is the only one among lemons, then the choice is not a problem for you. The choice is empowered by variety; when you kill variety, you eliminate choice. The only way to kill or eliminate variety is to reveal uniqueness. A unique line of a product will not have competition in the market. If you compete for a promotion in your office, it's because you have nothing unusual to offer in being in that position.

If what you can offer others can equally provide the same, then you will always face competition.

Variety is what is giving birth to choice and competition. In the case of Joseph, there was no competition for the position that Pharaoh proposed. If your gifts and talents lack uniqueness, you will die in the race for identity.

It is common for most footballers; gifted and talented but lack of rareness has thrown most of them into obscurity before manifestation. Dear reader, there are many hundreds of thousands of singers in the world today, but rareness is what makes Ron Kenoly, Don Moen, Kirk Franklin ring a bell in your mind.

Uniqueness is only revealed when you begin to see yourself as God sees you, and that is only possible by looking into the mirror of God's word. Combination of gift and wisdom is what makes you unique. "Can we find such a one as this is, a man in whom the Spirit of God is? Genesis 40:38.

Pharaoh asked this question trying to express what I'm saying in this section; without this question, several Egyptians would have thought themselves worthy of that task to which Joseph was put. Pharaoh, in no doubt, had several wise men and magicians that would have considered themselves deserving as they had many years of experience. When the problem is unique, only a unique person can bring about a unique solution, are you that person? Joseph was that person, and he ascended to the place of his dreams, the place where his brothers would come kneeling.

You're never too young or too old to improve your skills and qualifications. You must develop and maintain a heart that seeks to be better. You can increase your uniqueness by self-development. The world out there has many carbon copies, and you must strive to extricate all ambiguities for you to shine out your uniqueness.

Regular sharpening of your skills and acquisition of fresh and new skills must be a priority for you.

I believe by and large that one of the fundamental goals of education is to grow a person into their uniqueness. The knowledge we encounter in class or through other media clears from a person the clouds of popularity to reveal self to self.

Don't live a defeated life when inside you lay a champion eager to show up. Don't suffocate that giant. You are created for a solution that you alone can provide in the way you can provide. We are never meant to fit in but to stand out. That's why you rarely find people that look the same.

You are unique to God, and He is waiting for you to show forth what He has put in you. God spoke to Jeremiah and said, "Before I formed thee in the belly I knew thee, and before thou camest forth out of the womb I sanctified thee, and I ordained thee a prophet unto the nations." Jeremiah 1:5. God informs Jeremiah of his uniqueness. God didn't only create you; he sanctified (determined you for a particular assignment) and appointed him for the work of God's prophet to the nations. Likewise, you are not a meaningless creature roaming the earth but a unique treasure of God. You were born to stand out not to fit in.

Celebrating Uniqueness Is Not Arrogance

One of the things that cause people not to celebrate their uniqueness is the criticism of other people. There is a popular way of thinking that sponsors a false humility.

Usually, from a young age, we are told not to think highly of anything that makes you stand out. In the name of humility, a person is encouraged to denial any praise of character uniqueness.

It is wrong – people should be taught to be proud of anything in their personality and character that makes them one of a kind. We don't need to be arrogant but proud. Because of this fear instilled by sociality must people create an inner battle with themselves. Manprit Kaur gets it right in these words, "The most critical relationship in the world is the bond that you share with yourself. Are you comfortable being you or you're always trying to be someone else? Are you able to live up to your expectations or often end up feeling inadequate and incomplete?

Are you true to yourself and your dreams or you're trying to live someone else's definition of success? These are some vital questions you'd have to answer to determine how you feel about yourself and your life. We often see the world as a reflection of who we are. When you're relaxed and tranquil on the side, you will echo the same peace in all your relationships, begin by having an honest and fulfilling relationship with yourself."

To experience a healthy relationship with yourself, one of the cardinal appreciation you must have is an appreciation of your uniqueness. How do you know if you are arrogant about your uniqueness?

Watch out! Any time you begin to start having or revealing an exaggerated sense of your importance or abilities and belittle those who seem weak concerning your uniqueness, at that moment, you have gone into arrogance. But should you beat yourself all in the name of fear of the trap of arrogance? No! We need to know that others, just like us, have individual uniqueness; therefore, we should strive to accommodate, accept, and allow them to be themselves.

Every time you become too critical of your uniqueness, you begin to deny or pretend that you are somebody you are not. Many people are in search of an authentic self, looking to every other place, and people while they keep bypassing themselves.

Your true self will always bother you till you gather the courage to let your authentic-self go loose. You must realize that every time you live by what other people's expectations of you, you are missing out on something important – YOU.

Borrowing The Neighbor's Vessel

There is a story I love so much; it is that of a widow who was about to lose her two boys to her late husband's creditors. All she had was a little jar of oil in the house. By the instruction of Elisha, she borrowed vessels into which she poured her little oil.

She gathered as many vessels as she could find from her neighbors, and each of them was filled up. The little oil was poured into many containers; that is the miracle of borrowing vessels.

Your uniqueness may be like that little oil. There are people out there who have several vessels that you can use to pour your oil into. The little oil in a little jar can multiply to fill many vessels.

Your uniqueness expressed on the platform of other people can be multiplied and advertised.

Another man's vessel may be a social platform, goodwill, recommendation, etc. out there are people whose gifts, talents, abilities can help globalize your uniqueness.

In the words of Anthony J. D'Angelo, "Don't reinvent the wheel, just realign it."

Pouring your little into other people's vessel also speaks of building on the successes and achievements of other people. If you try to do everything, you may not live long enough to get to a point where everything is in place to start working on your dreams. You don't have to start making vessels when people around you have already done that.

Berners-Lee unknown to many people is the unsung or at least under-sung hero of the information age. This is the man who invented the Worldwide Web (WWW). If I were the one, I would have probably named this modern miracle as 'MAZ' for Mudolo Andrew Zadok.

Surprisingly, most of the wealth and fame emanating from this invention have gone to people other than Tim Berners-Lee.

At some point, Berners-Lee owned a 13-year-old Volkswagen Rabbit for his vehicle and lived a simplicity type of life.

I won't bore with much detail, the lesson here is how a man has bought into this world something so significant without demanding accolades and monetary rewards.

I say, "If you pioneer any path, don't leave spikes and thorns. Greatness is not that you cleared the path but that others can walk the path". Can you do something even if it means others will get rich by it excluding you? Some of my favorite quotes by Berners-Lee are:

1. "When I invented the web, I didn't have to ask anyone's permission. Now, hundreds of millions of people are using it freely."

2. "The web is more a social creation than a technical one. I designed it for a social effect — to help people work together — and not as a technical toy."

I want you to notice something in these quotes –

'PEOPLE.'

Berners-Lee offered his vessel for others who had nothing significant apart from a little idea. People matter and they should matter to you as well. Let others ride on your vessel (uniqueness).

All the online businesses owe their success to the invention of one man. People don't have to create the internet all they need is to use what already exists to build their dream.

Mark Zuckerberg's Facebook was launched on the wings of Berners-Lee creation. Berners-Lee product created China's richest man; Jack Ma. There are many people out there who became millionaires in US dollars by borrowing Berners-Lee's vessel. You too can become great by pouring your uniqueness into someone else vessel.

Never look down on yourself; you need to celebrate every gift, talent, or an ability that sets you apart from other people. To go above and beyond the huddles of life to achieve your dreams and purpose, you need to aware of your true self. Revolt from living the life that other people dictate for you – find your space and reign in that place; you are unique!

"If everyone would look for that
uniqueness then we would have a very

colorful world" – Michael Schenker

CHAPTER SEVENTEEN

THE TEST OF FORGIVENESS

*"Unforgiveness is like drinking poison yourself
and waiting for the other person to die" –
Marianne Williamson*

In an Indian farming community, families depended on each other for social, moral, and financial support. With time, one farmer insulted his neighbor over a dispute regarding that season's farming implements. After the whole bitter confrontation, they all went to their respective homes fuming with anger. When the one who insulted went home and couldn't sleep that night. His was troubled. There's was a community of happiness and cordial relations. Should this one misunderstanding disturb the peace of the community? Upon realizing his mistake, he resolved to go to his fellow to ask for forgiveness. When the morrow came, and the offender was now asking for forgiveness, his fellow farmer paused for a while thinking what to do.

The Offended farmer told him to take a bag of feathers and drop them in the center of town. The farmer did as he was told to the amazement of many passers-by.

Then the offended farmer asked him to go and collect the feathers and put them back in the bag. The farmer tried but couldn't as the feathers had all blown away. When he returned with the empty container, the offended farmer said, "The same thing is true about your words. You dropped them rather easily, but you cannot retrieve them, so be very careful in choosing your words". And the offended farmer went away. Did the offending farmer receive forgiveness? Well, this story saves to show you and me that in life offense are bound to happen; either you offend or be offended. To transgress is easy but to forgive is hard.

As Shelley Emling rightly opines, "Sometimes it takes every fiber of your being to forgive someone." Yes, forgiveness is a must, but the question is this: do some people deserve to be forgiven? Well, the famous thought suggests that some wrongs are just too grave to be ignored and the perpetrator should not be forgiven. It is often suggested that some offenses can be forgiven while others should not be forgiven.

Let me share a story before I recollect the story of Joseph. Mercy was a tough girl. We met in college, and everyone was in trouble if you dared intrude into her personal space.

Mercy was stunningly beautified with a striking smile that just swept many boys off their feet. I was peculiarly drawn to her in a normal friendship.

It was not a romantic relationship but a cordial friendship. We were close. I notice that every man she would date was always married. Even though many guys in her age bracket made efforts to date her, they failed repeatedly.

I remember nostalgically calling her to my cabin and confronting her about the partner I suspected in her relationship.

"It's nothing," she insisted. When I probed a little further, she broke down in hysteria demanding to leave. I was not about to give that easily. "I know it hurts… I'm so sorry," I said, putting my hand on her shoulder for reassurance.

It happened that during her childhood, her father repeatedly abused her sexually. She hated him with pure hatred and any person that resembled him just ignited her goal. Enduring those humiliating, pain encounters of abuse cause Mercy to make a resolve; she would never be a victim of any man and to ensure that she planned instead to inflict pain on every man that proposed love to her. She would readily accept a proposal from any married man; students, lecturers, business people, politicians as long as he was married. She would demand a lot from the man so much so that he abandoned his wife and children. Then when the man had invested all his heart into the relationship, he would drop him unapologetically. The look on the faces of the men gave her a sense of fulfillment, and she enjoyed the drama the men would act out in the hope of winning her back.

Sadly, the man who abused her died many years before she came to college.

The moment she saw another happy family man, the pain revived, and she would be so depressed. Her purpose in life was all about getting back at the man who abused her.

She didn't allow herself to love any man. And when her emotions let her down, and she fell in love, she would quickly abandon the relationship. Well, her story concludes that we acted out roles; I became the father that abused her.

She had to pour out all her pain and frustrations, and she sat there and cried, saying sorry. It was a moving scene.

I asked for forgiveness, and she released the pain she carried from childhood. Today Mercy is happily married, and yes, she protects her family with all heart.

Another story is of a European couple that loved each other. James and Janet were the envy of their community. The luxurious lifestyle they lived made them a spectacle. Their love was true love. Janet had so much trust in the husband, and she reached a point where her man was a saint. Even when they were drifting apart, she couldn't see it. On the other hand, James was going through a phase of loneliness, but all was well with Janet. Occasionally he'd tried to table his secret struggles with her, but she hashed him saying, "Perhaps you are just worked up honey, It will pass." Well, it didn't pass; James started having extramarital affairs. Infidelity had crept into their happy marriage. After a while of his secret life, James couldn't bear the guilt; he sought help from his local pastor.

And after overcoming his secret struggles, James finally confessed to Janet. He was very apologetic and begged for forgiveness, But Janet didn't want to hear any of it.

Janet was so heartbroken and filed for divorce.

Even when divorce went through; each one going his own way, Janet still couldn't find it in her heart to forgive James. She stopped going out of her home, stopped picking calls; she shut herself in a sauna of grief. She died a year later of depression. Meanwhile, James had forgiven himself and went on to marry his secretary with whom he fathered two kids.

What Is Unforgiveness?

Unlike Mercy and James, Janet failed the test of

forgiveness. While Mercy went above and beyond the pain of sexual abuse, Janet was unable to excel above and beyond infidelity. What is Unforgiveness? Unforgiveness is a failure to stop feeling angry or resentful towards (someone) for an offense or mistake. Well, many people know that Unforgiveness is not right, and Marianne Williamson puts it well; "Unforgiveness is like drinking poison yourself and waiting for the other person to die." Quality empirical research has shown that Unforgiveness increases levels of stress, tension, levels of depression, and many other emotions that can lead to health problems; problems such as heart disease. The hard fact is this, knowing that Unforgiveness is terrible and does not in any way make it easy to release hurts and forgive.

When we take offense, we are looking for sympathy, revenge, justice, and punishment for the offender. When we don't seem to get the truth, we think we deserve and the offender is let loose, anger is developed in our hearts. Anger is toxic to you, and in no way does it harm the other person.

Let us turn to Joseph's story: Genesis 50:17-21.

"So shall ye say unto Joseph, Forgive, I pray thee now, the trespass of thy brethren, and their sin; for they did unto thee evil: and now, we pray thee, forgive the trespass of the servants of the God of thy father. And Joseph wept when they spake unto him.

And his brethren also went and fell down before his face; and they said, Behold, we be thy servants.

And Joseph said unto them, Fear not: for am I in the place of God?

But as for you, ye thought evil against me; but God meant it unto good, to bring to pass, as it is this day, to save many people alive. Now, therefore, fear ye not: I will nourish you, and your little ones. And he comforted them, and spake kindly unto them".

How can you handle betrayal, rejection, commodification, accusation, and imprisonment? All those experience sponsor a lot of anger in many people's lives. That anger can be so disastrous and can limit your destiny. Let us see some critical lesson in how Joseph handled his heart. He forgave!

1.   **He heard**: Joseph gave audience and a chance for his brothers to express themselves. If you want to deal with Unforgiveness, you must be willing to provide an opportunity for the offender to speak his mind and apologize. Most people never give a chance to their offenders; they don't want to hear anything. This is the first step to forgiving your offender. *Listen*!

2.   **He cried**: Sometimes, the pain you will feel will be so intense that the only way you can gain relief is by bursting into tears. Crying or grieving over something or someone gives you comfort. When you shed tears, you are opening a pressure release valve. Don't pretend to be fine; sometimes you've got to let your frustration, disappointment, and hurt come out. *Cry*!

3.   **He released**: Joseph was able to let go of the pain and bitterness of betrayal. When his father and brothers expected revenge, Joseph went above and beyond his pain and embraced his brothers with tears; not tears of frustration and bitterness but love and reassurance. To overcome Unforgiveness, one has to let go of the pain even though the memories may linger. Suspend all forms of insidious plots against your offenders. Don't begin to curse them, saying; they shall see no good thing in life or that their days shall be cut short rather wish them well. Release!

4.   **He comforted**: Alexander Pope says, "To err is human; to forgive, divine." Joseph's brothers knew that he was just but human; would he forgive them? Well, Joseph was a human but one touched by the divine. His brothers felt guilty, shame, undeserving of favor but deserving punishment. Joseph made his brothers feel comfortable. Comfort!

5.   **He nourished**: How can you know you've forgiven someone? Imagine a baby; it needs the mother's milk for full nutrition for wholesome growth. In the same manner, if you have forgiven someone, you will do what is in your power to build, encourage, and promote a holistic life for them. You will not wish them harm but well. You will warn them when their impending danger. You will protect them from malice and any other thing. When you are harboring anger, grudges, and hatred in your heart, it's almost always you'll wish harm to those responsible for your hurt. Do all you can to build your offenders; when they ask and when you see the need. Nourish.

Out of the five steps, I have given you will observe that the first three steps are for the victim's benefit and the last two are for the benefit of the offender.

I need to emphasize that forgiveness does more good to you than to the offender.

The last two may be accepted or rejected by the offender when offered, but that should not deter you. Once you have completed the first three steps, then you can succeed in doing the last 2.

"Anger makes you smaller, while forgiveness forces you to grow beyond what you were" – Cherie Carter-Scott

Forgiveness is the test of arrival in your dreamland. You

are not yet successful until you can look at those who offended you on your way; intentional and voluntary release all ill feelings; drop all negative attitudes and have the heart to see your offenders better.

Why won't you forgive?

The pain of betrayal was just too intense.

The damage done was irreversible

The Abuse of your rights was inexcusable.

The list of excuses for failure to forgive is endless. It is as long as the possible offense that can exist. Most often, we all legitimatize the reason for your inability to forgive. Friend, no reason is legitimate enough for you to fail to forgive.

Come to think of it; there is only one reason for failure to forgive: you think you are better than those seeking forgiveness from you.

When it dawns on you, the offenses you have committed and are yet to commit, you will readily forgive and release others. You too, need forgiveness! (See; Mark 11:26).

The other reason for Unforgiveness is a lack of willingness to admit a wrong by the offender. This is crucial for most people. Do you only forgive when the offender asks for forgiveness? What if they deny any wrongdoing and therefore never ask for forgiveness?

If you are harboring Unforgiveness, stop waiting for your offender to ask for forgiveness. You forgive them.

Whether the offender asks for it or not; forgiveness must always be your option in the event of an offense. Yes, you are allowed to grieve, to get angry and then after it all you must forgive!

There is a lot of debuts around this question. Have you forgiven if you haven't forgotten? Can you forgive and forget? However, you want to phrase the question the truth remains; forgiveness is essential for good health. About forgetting, well, it is my conviction that to wipe clean one's memory of a painful episode of their lives may not be possible, but it is possible to wipe clean their emotions of the anger, bitterness, and grudges of an episode of pain.

Finding Forgiveness

The truth remains, it is easy to offend, and it is harder to forgive. "When we forgive, we free ourselves from the bitter ties that bind us to the one who hurts us" – Claire Frazier-Yzaguirre.

Furthermore, it is even harder to forgive a friend or family member than an enemy. It pains a lot to be offended by a loved one; say infidelity in a marriage. We must recognize that forgiveness plays a vital role in the maintenance of healthy social relationships; thus, for us to have peaceful communities, we must seek the path of forgiveness.

Many are the offenses on the way to your dreams; you must learn to forgive. When you have forgiven, you have passed the crucial test on the journey to your destiny. You are only successful when you forgive!

CHAPTER EIGHTEEN

FINISHING WELL

"To become 'unique,' the challenge is to fight the hardest battle which anyone can imagine until you reach your destination" – A. P. J. Abdul Kalam

No one has a problem with the first mile. Even an infant could do fine for a while. But it isn't the start that matters. It's the finish line. How true these words of Julien Smith. Everyone is a hero at the starting line, but only those who endure to the finish line are true heroes, they are the crowned heroes. Most people strive to make a good first impression but seem to fall short in the process of time. As much as first impressions are essential, what will matter is the last impression people have of you. Most heroes in history hard significant character flaws but they are celebrated nonetheless because of finishing well.

Nelson Mandela once said that "I was called a terrorist yesterday, but when I came out of jail, many people embraced me, including my enemies, and that is what I normally tell other people who say those who are struggling for liberation in their country are terrorists." It is his finish that made Mandela an icon to be emulated. You must always look to your end because that is what will define whether you lived successfully or not. No man can be called great, happy, or prosperous until he goes to the grave. Whatever forms of achievement a person scores in his lifetime should be only viewed as indicators of a successful end. Thus each individual must work hard to stay on the path that point to a strong finish. Any claim of success is arrogant and misguided. History has demonstrated time without number that men whom we thought to be successful failed at the eleventh hour. The point I'm making here is that we all must remain humble and not be puffed up by any score of achievement. Of course, we should celebrate our scores but never let them get to our heads and hearts. Let me call to your remembrance the words of Paul in writing to Timothy (See; 2 Timothy 4:7). At this juncture, I would like to dive in a little deeper in those words of Paul: "I have fought a good fight, I have finished my course, I have kept the faith." There are three keys to finishing well that we can learn from the words of Paul:

Fight the Good Fight

Football icon Lionel Messi says, "You have to fight to

reach your dream. You have to sacrifice and work hard for it. Life is a fight.

Messi shows us that fighting for your dream does not in any way infer the use of physical weapons, but it's fighting through the avenues of hard work and sacrifice.

Friends, it is better to fight for something than to live nothing.

To finish well, you need to be a fighter. Many forces will fight your dream in life; forces of jealous, negative criticism, discouragements, and disappointments, rejection, lack of resources, etc. Friends, you must be courageous to face the blows that life throws at you. You can't afford to give up. What is even more impressive is resistance will not only come externally but also from within. Your mind, body, and will, at times, will prove to be stubborn. There is a need for discipline to win the fights that originate from within. For example, moods can be a huge impediment to your fight for your dreams. Frank Herbert puts it well when he says "What has 'mood' to do with it? You fight when the necessity arises, no matter the mood! Mood's a thing for cattle or making love or playing the baliset. It's not for fighting.

Fight until you win!

Fight until you achieve!

Fight until you have!

Fight to the last drop of blood!

"The resistance that you fight physically in the gym and the resistance that you fight in life can only build a strong character," these words were said by Arnold Schwarzenegger.

The implication being that resistance (fight) you engage in will produce a strong character as long as you don't give in. Most people don't like to fight; there is a lot of energy one must summon when going for a fight, and if he/she is not willing to sacrifice, they will not fight. If you are going to go above and beyond, you will be required to fight.

So settle that in your psychic. Fight the good fight. The good fight is the fight for your dream and not someone else's. The good fight is that fight for your purpose. Friends fight the good fight. Life is full of mountains and valleys, and if you are going to go above and beyond them, you have to fight else you can forget about your dream.

Finish The Course

Success varies; what you can success may be just a mid-point for another person. In the journey of life, you must realize that it is ok to be inspired by other people but not to accept inferiority. Your mission is different. Allow me to cite a famous proverb which says, "Every morning in Africa, a gazelle wakes up. It knows it must outrun the fastest lion or it will be killed. Every morning in Africa, a lion wakes up. It knows it must run faster than the slowest gazelle, or it will starve. It doesn't matter whether you're the lion or a gazelle – when the sun comes up, you'd better be running."

You are not the African gazelle; you are alive to outdo other people; neither are you the African lion to survive by outshining other people.

Life is not about outdoing others; it's about finishing your own course. You concerned must be your race.

Are you running your race or perhaps you've moved into someone else's race?

Make a firm resolve not to compete with others. Mike Fanelli said, "I tell our runners to divide the race into thirds. Run the first part with your head, the middle part with your personality, and the last part with your heart."

I want to agree with Mike that just as he advises his runners, the same counsel is what I'm advancing to you, my friend. Start the race with the head first, personality second and thirdly your heart.

- **Head First**: Zig Ziglar with whom I agree says, "If you don't see yourself as a winner, then you cannot perform as a winner." It all must begin with a mental conception. If your mind can hold, then your hand won't hold it in reality. Those who succeed don't succeed by accident, but their success has been a function of hard mental work. Planning and strategizing always produce success. Like Benjamin Franklin affirms, "If you fail to plan, you are planning to fail." You cannot replace the function of planning and expect to succeed. Prayer, fasting, charity, and any other thing cannot be substitutes for planning. To finish well remember – Head First.

- **Personality Second**: Denis Waitley says that "The winner's edge is not in a gifted birth, a high IQ, or in talent. The winner's edge is all in the attitude, not aptitude. Attitude is the criterion for success. The Concise Oxford English Dictionary (Eleventh Edition) defines personality as "The combination of characteristics or qualities that form an individual's distinctive character." To finish well, you need to work on your character. Character flaws have been the undoing of many great destinies. Indeed, talent can't take your place, but the character will keep you there. You must cultivate attributes that sponsor winners; Attitude, Persistence, Hard work, Critical thinking, and many other characteristics. Depending on your field of endeavor, you need to identify indispensable qualities that will make you a winner no matter what. Cultivate them, and continuous improvement on them. To finish well remember – Personality Second.

• **Thirdly, Heart**: Blaise Pascal made a remarkable statement I would like to insert here; he said: "The heart has its reason which reason does not know." Your heart is the most magnificent campus you possess; therefore, you should never go anywhere without it; everywhere you go, go with your heart. There is an inner witness in our hearts about everything we want to do or are doing. To finish well, you must pay attention to that inner voice of your conscious. Yes, it is prudent to listen from other people, but care must be given not to let what you feel in your heart be trumped upon. Many a time, people have poorly ended because they cared so much about the opinion of the masses and despite the voice of reason in their heart. People are there to confirm what we already hold in our hearts. To finish well remember – Thirdly, Heart.

Keep the Faith

Our lives are governed by value sets and beliefs, consciously, or unconsciously.

We all hold specific values that determine the decision and choices we make in everyday life. It is the values and beliefs that define people. Keeping the faith, therefore, implies staying true to those core values and belief that have governed your life to success.

You must hold to a high moral code. The danger of success is that it presents opportunities to lose critical moral values. The richest man in the world, Bill Gates says, "Success is a lousy teacher. It seduces smart people into thinking they can't lose". I have observed with sadness how individual businesspeople will castigate customers forgetting that they have succeeded in business because of those customers. Mr. Gates is right; you can lose after winning. Therefore our focus should not only be on winning and achieving in life but much more on FINISHING WELL.

The Pinnacle of Success

Winning, Succeeding, and anything that denotes excellent achievement in life must be embraced rightly, or it may corrupt even a saint. The word "win" by implication, connotes comparison, and competition. Today there are many movements birthed around the theme of being a winner.

From early childhood, we are encouraged to be first; work hard and be number one. I'm not one of those who say ever since I was a kid, and I was always the winner.

The great mistake most people make is that they fall in the trap of competing with other people instead of winning against failure to achieve personal goals.

Don't make outdoing another person your goal. Often when you meet old friends the everyday talk; "where is so and so, what are they doing, are they married, and so on… The best thing your friend's success and achievement can do for you is inspiration.

But if you get in the competition, you may end up being disappointed with yourself.

Let me summarize this book with want I believe to be the best view of success. Drawing strength from the words of Larry Bird who said, "A winner is someone who recognizes his God-given talents, works his tail off to develop them into skills, and uses these skills to accomplish his goals." There are various points of reflection I want us to focus on as we appreciate Larry Birds words:

1. **Recognizing God-given talents**: A winner, therefore, is an individual who has come to appreciate his unique God-given talents or gift. One of the dangers in life is that it is possible to succeed in doing the wrong. You've got realize that you are only successful to the extent that sticks to God-given assignment. I have already shown you that the purest of dreams is often the dreams we have in

early childhood, but as we grow, we lose it because of the apparent challenges. People often damn their God-given gifts for mere survival and forsake their dreams. You only win in life when you recognize your God-given endowments.

2.   **Work your tail to develop them**: Hard work, coupled with smart work, always produces winners. I always advise people that recognition of potential, talent, gifts, etc. is only the first step. You've got to work hard to make that your expertise and gift is developed to a level that people can demand it. Frequency of use will give you the edge you require to be on top of your game. Many people wait to be paid for using their talent, and as a result, they remain stranded all their lives. Development of your gift entails that you perfect it – mastery. Vince Lombardi says, "Practice does not make perfect, perfect practice makes perfect." Work hard and smart to perfect your talent and gift.

3.   **Use the skill to accomplish yourgoals**: The talents and gifts God gave you are for the accomplishment of your purpose. Your life is not an accident, and thus you don't live by guesswork. You are not inadequate for the purpose and life you must live. You have all the talents and gifts. All that remains for you to do is to sharped them and direct

them to the direction of your goals. What are your life goals? You must realize that you have all it takes to attain them, discover and develop your God-given talents, gifts, and potentials.

EPILOGUE

"Sometimes it's the journey that teaches you a lot about your destination" – Drake

Joseph's journey to destiny is not unique to him; you also have a mission. On this journey you may decide to take the easy way, the normal way, or the divine way; the difference in the route you choose will determine firstly, the TIME of arrival. Joseph journey took over ten years for him to arrive in the place of his purpose. Secondly, the route you take will determine your CHARACTER on arrival. Many people have fallen because of a lack of character. Only the divine route will develop the character required to take and keep you in the place of your purpose. Thirdly, the route you take to your destiny will determine the size of your HEART. Individual destinies undoubtedly require a big heart that could accommodate people of various sorts; a heart with a capacity to wave off all manner of wrongs and embrace peace. A heart that is ready to embrace reconciliation and discard revengeful insinuations. Erol Ozan says, "Some beautiful paths can't be discovered without getting lost." Do you think Joseph understood the episodes of his life? Joseph like you may have often felt lost and with no sense of direction. But you don't have despair; it is just another stop on the journey to your destiny.

Let me conclude with the thoughts of other people on the subject:

"Life is a journey that must be traveled no matter how bad the roads and accommodations" — Oliver Goldsmith

Success is a journey, not a destination. The doing is often more important than the outcome — Arthur Ashe

"Transformation is a process, and as life happens, there are tons of ups and downs. It's a journey of discovery — there are moments on mountaintops and moments in deep valleys of despair" — Rick Warren

"Focus on the journey, not the destination. Joy is found not in finishing an activity but in doing it"— Greg Anderson

"To get the most out of a life's journey, one has to positively live through its humbling and glorious circumstances" — Wayne Chirisa

"I may not have gone where I intended to go, but I think I have ended up where I intended to be" — Douglas Adams

"An adventure is only an inconvenience rightly considered. An inconvenience is only an adventure wrongly considered" — G. K. Chesterton

The road of life twists and turns, and no two directions are ever the same. Yet our lessons come from the journey, not the destination" — Don Williams, Jr.

"We don't receive wisdom; we must discover it for ourselves after a journey that no one can take for us or spare us" – Marcel Proust

"To get where you want to go you can't only do what you like" — Peter Abrahams

"If all difficulties were known at the outset of a long journey, most of us would never start at all" — Dan Rather

"Every journey has an end" — Seneca

No matter your trouble, remain true to yourself, hold your values, and stand for your beliefs. In utilizing your God-given endowments for the benefit of other men, you will be rewarded with a high sense of purpose. Your purpose is beyond you – purpose goes beyond your comfort. It is the state of being blessed to bless. Within you are all the potentials, you require to achieve your purpose. Your first work is to discover, develop, and use them. Your potential is like a diamond in the rough – most people have exceptional qualities and possibilities but lack refinement thus the requirement of passing through the process of polishing. It will hurt, you will be under pressure, and at the end you will emerge a lustrous fit for your life purpose. Therefore don't whine when you go through the rough time because they are the cutters that remove the raw edges of in your life.

HELPING YOU REVEAL YOUR WEALTHY AND GLORY:

By Andrew Mudolo

References

https://www.thestreet.com/story/11173382/1/10-people-living-the-american-dream.html

https://www.psychologytoday.com/articles/200507/advice-stopping-pain-the-past

https://www.hsutx.edu/Hall-of-Leaders/Virginia-(Boyd)-Connally (Accessed 22nd September 2017).

https://www.cnbc.com/2017/05/31/14-billionaires-signed-bill-gates-and-warren-buffetts-giving-pledge.htm

http://www.celebzen.com/13-celebs-who-were-once-broke-and-homeless/5/

https://addicted2success.com/news/10-succesful-people-who-proved-that-age-is-nothing-but-a-number/ (accessed 9 October 2017)

Africa's Most Promising Young Entrepreneurs: Forbes Africa 30 under 30 for 2015. http://www.forbes.com (accessed 14 October 2017)

https://www.psychologytoday.com/blog/fulfillment-any-age/201201/15-wise-and-inspiring-quotes-about-aging (accessed 13 October 2017)

https://www.brainpickings.org/2016/02/08/mendeleev-periodic-table-dream/ (Accessed: 4 October 2017) https://www.psychologytoday.com/articles/201403/dreams-glory (accessed 18 March 2017)

http://www.psychologytoday.com/blog/fixing-families/201502/the-ideal-family-how-do-you-stuck (accessed 12 October 2017)

http://www.adweek.com/tvspy/oprah-on-her-time-at-wjz-humiliated-embarrassed-and-sexually-harassed/11382

http://www.pnas.org/content/108/15/6270.full.pdf

http://www.inc.com/bill-murphy-jr/11-inspiring-people-who-lost-it-all-and-came-back-stronger.html   (accessed: December 14, 2016)

https://m.indiatimes.com/lifestyle/self/false-accusations-of-rape-295920.html (accessed 18 October 2017)

http://www.express.co.uk/news/uk/618874/late-bloomers-sixty-plus-greatest-achievements-Judi-Dench-Karl-Lagerfield-Ranulph-Fiennes (Accessed 9 October 2017)

http://www.celebzen.com/13-celebs-who-were-once-broke-and-homeless/5/   (Accessed 12 September 2017).

https://childdevelopmentinfo.com/development/7-ways-to-encourage-your-childs-uniqueness/ (accessed 16 October 2017)

Welcome to EditPad.org - your online plain text editor. Enter or paste your text here. To download and save it, click on the button below.